10th Workshop on Asian Language Resources

Held at the 24th International Conference on Computational Linguistics (COLING 2012)

Mumbai, India
9 December 2012

Editors:

Rachel Edita O. Roxas
Ruvan Weerasinghe
Sarmad Hussain
Virach Sornlertamvanich

ISBN: 978-1-62748-353-7

Printed from e-media with permission by:

Curran Associates, Inc.
57 Morehouse Lane
Red Hook, NY 12571

CURRAN ASSOCIATES INC.
proceedings.com

Some format issues inherent in the e-media version may also appear in this print version.

Printed by Curran Associates, Inc. (2013)

Association for Computational Linguistics
209 N. Eighth Street
Stroudsburg, Pennsylvania 18360

Phone: 1-570-476-8006
Fax: 1-570-476-0860

acl@aclweb.org

Additional copies of this publication are available from:

Curran Associates, Inc.
57 Morehouse Lane
Red Hook, NY 12571 USA
Phone: 845-758-0400
Fax: 845-758-2634
Email: curran@proceedings.com
Web: www.proceedings.com

COLING 2012

24th International Conference on Computational Linguistics

Proceedings of the 10th Workshop on Asian Language Resources

Workshop chairs:
Ruvan Weerasinghe, Sarmad Hussain,
Virach Sornlertlamvanich and Rachel Edita O. Roxas

09 December 2012
Mumbai, India

Diamond sponsors

Tata Consultancy Services
Linguistic Data Consortium for Indian Languages (LDC-IL)

Gold Sponsors

Microsoft Research
Beijing Baidu Netcon Science Technology Co. Ltd.

Silver sponsors

IBM, India Private Limited
Crimson Interactive Pvt. Ltd.
Yahoo
Easy Transcription & Software Pvt. Ltd.

Preface

As research in the field of Natural Language Processing matures across Asia, there is a growing need for developing language resources. However the region is not only short in linguistic resources for the more than 2200 language spoken in the region, there is also lack of experience of the researchers to develop these resources. As the efforts to develop the linguistic resources increases, there is also need to coordinate the efforts to develop common frameworks and processes so that these resources can be used by those dealing with new and under-resourced languages.

The Asian Language Resources Workshop (ALR) is organised under the Asian Federation of Natural Language Processing (AFNLP) to chart and catalogue the status of Asian Language Resources, to investigate and discuss the problems related to the standards and specification of creating and sharing various levels of language resources, to promote a dialogue between developers and users of various language resources in order to address any gaps in language resources and practical applications, and to nurture collaboration in their development, and to provide the opportunity for researchers from Asia to collaborate with researchers in other regions.

We are very pleased to publish this volume that contains the papers presented at the Tenth Workshop on Asian Language Resources (ALR-10) held in conjunction with the 24th International Conference on Computational Linguistics (COLING 2012) from 8th to 15th December 2012 in Mumbai, India. We received a total of 25 submissions for resources and tools for languages in the region such as Persian, Tibetan, Urdu, Mongolian, Assamese, Bodo, Magahi, Korean, Hindi and Bangla, of which 14 (56%) have been accepted for oral presentation through a double-blind refereeing process. We would like to thank the authors for their submissions and the Program Committee for their timely reviews. We hope that ALR workshops will continue to encourage researchers to focus on developing and sharing resources for Asian languages, an essential requirement for research in NLP in the region.

Ruvan Weerasinghe (Chair)
Sarmad Hussain (Co-Chair)
Virach Sornlertlamvanich (Co-Chair)
Rachel Edita O. Roxas (Co-Chair)

Organizing Committee

Organizers:

Ruvan Weerasinghe, University of Colombo School of Computing, Sri Lanka
Sarmad Hussain, University of Engineering and Technology, Pakistan
Virach Sornlertlamvanich, NECTEC, Thailand
Rachel Roxas, De La Salle University, Philippines

Program Committee:

Abid Khan, Univ. of Peshawar, Pakistan
Chai Wutiwiwatchai - NECTEC, Thailand
Dipti Misra Sharma, IIIT, Hyderabad, India
Francis Bond, Nanyang Technological University, Singapore
Haizhou Li - I2R, Singapore
Key-Sun Choi - KAIST, Korea
Kiyoaki Shirai - JAIST, Japan
Miriam Butt – Univ. of Konstanz, Germany
Mirna Adriani – Univ. of Indonesia, Indonesia
Rachel Edita O. Roxas – De La Salle University, Philippines
Rajeev Sangal, IIIT Hyderabad, India
Reinhard Schaler – Localization Research Centre, University of Limerick, Ireland
Ruli Marunung – Univ. of Indonesia, Indonesia
Ruvan Weerasinghe - LTRL, University of Colombo, School of Computing, Sri Lanka
Sarmad Hussain – CLE-KICS, UET Lahore, Pakistan
Steven Bird – University of Melbourne, Australia
Takenobu Tokunaga - Tokyo Institute of Technology, Japan
Virach Sornlertlamvanich - NECTEC, Thailand

Table of Contents

Korean NLP2RDF Resources
YoungGyun Hahm, KyungTae Lim, Jungyeul Park, Yongun Yoon and Key-Sun Choi 1

Building Large Scale Text Corpus for Tibetan Natural Language Processing by Extracting Text from Web Pages
Huidan Liu, Minghua Nuo, Jian Wu and Yeping He 11

A Structured Approach for Building Assamese Corpus: Insights, Applications and Challenges
Prof. Shikhar Kr. Sarma, Himadri Bharali, Ambeswar Gogoi, Ratul Deka and Anup Kr Barman 21

Corpus Building of Literary Lesser Rich Language-Bodo: Insights and Challenges
Biswajit Brahma, Anup Kr. Barman, Prof. Shikhar Kr. Sarma and Bhatima Boro 29

Dependency Parsers for Persian
Mojgan Seraji, Beáta Megyesi and Joakim Nivre 35

A New DOP Model for Phrase-structure Parsing of Persian Sentences
Zahra Sarabi and Morteza Analoui 45

A Hybrid Dependency Parser for Bangla
Arnab Dhar, Sanjay Chatterji, Sudeshna Sarkar and Anupam Basu 55

Repairing Bengali Verb Chunks for Improved Bengali to Hindi Machine Translation
Sanjay Chatterji, Nabanita Datta, Arnab Dhar, Biswanath Barik, Sudeshna Sarkar and Anupam Basu 65

Domain Specific Ontology Extractor For Indian Languages
Brijesh Bhatt and Pushpak Bhattacharyya 75

Constrained Hidden Markov Model for Bilingual Keyword Pairs Alignment
Denny Cahyadi, Fabien Cromieres and Sadao Kurohashi 85

N-gram and Gazetteer List Based Named Entity Recognition for Urdu: A Scarce Resourced Language
Faryal Jahangir, Waqas Anwar, Usama Ijaz Bajwa and Xuan Wang 95

Developing a POS tagger for Magahi: A Comparative Study
Ritesh Kumar, Bornini Lahiri and Deepak Alok 105

Enhancing Lemmatization for Mongolian and its Application to Statistical Machine Translation
Chimeddorj Odbayar and Atsushi Fujii 115

Translations of Ambiguous Hindi Pronouns to Possible Bengali Pronouns
Sanjay Chatterji, Sudeshna Sarkar and Anupam Basu 125

10th Workshop on Asian Language Resources
Program

Sunday, 9 December 2012

	Session 1 – Linguistic Resources
09:00–09:30	*Korean NLP2RDF Resources* YoungGyun Hahm, KyungTae Lim, Jungyeul Park, Yongun Yoon and Key-Sun Choi
09:30–10:00	*Building Large Scale Text Corpus for Tibetan Natural Language Processing by Extracting Text from Web Pages* Huidan Liu, Minghua Nuo, Jian Wu and Yeping He
10:00–10:30	*A Structured Approach for Building Assamese Corpus: Insights, Applications and Challenges* Prof. Shikhar Kr. Sarma, Himadri Bharali, Ambeswar Gogoi, Ratul Deka and Anup Kr Barman
10:30–11:00	*Corpus Building of Literary Lesser Rich Language-Bodo: Insights and Challenges* Biswajit Brahma, Anup Kr. Barman, Prof. Shikhar Kr. Sarma and Bhatima Boro
11:00–11:30	Tea break
	Session 2 – Morphology and Syntax Parsing
11:30–12:00	*Dependency Parsers for Persian* Mojgan Seraji, Beáta Megyesi and Joakim Nivre
12:00–12:30	*A New DOP Model for Phrase-structure Parsing of Persian Sentences* Zahra Sarabi and Morteza Analoui
12:30–13:00	*A Hybrid Dependency Parser for Bangla* Arnab Dhar, Sanjay Chatterji, Sudeshna Sarkar and Anupam Basu
13:00–13:30	*Repairing Bengali Verb Chunks for Improved Bengali to Hindi Machine Translation* Sanjay Chatterji, Nabanita Datta, Arnab Dhar, Biswanath Barik, Sudeshna Sarkar and Anupam Basu
13:30–14:30	Lunch

Sunday, 9 December 2012 (continued)

Session 3 – Knowledge Extraction

14:30–15:00 *Domain Specific Ontology Extractor For Indian Languages*
Brijesh Bhatt and Pushpak Bhattacharyya

15:00–15:30 *Constrained Hidden Markov Model for Bilingual Keyword Pairs Alignment*
Denny Cahyadi, Fabien Cromieres and Sadao Kurohashi

15:30–16:00 *N-gram and Gazetteer List Based Named Entity Recognition for Urdu: A Scarce Resourced Language*
Faryal Jahangir, Waqas Anwar, Usama Ijaz Bajwa and Xuan Wang

16:00–16:30 Tea break

Session 4 – Applications

16:30–17:00 *Developing a POS tagger for Magahi: A Comparative Study*
Ritesh Kumar, Bornini Lahiri and Deepak Alok

17:00–17:30 *Enhancing Lemmatization for Mongolian and its Application to Statistical Machine Translation*
Chimeddorj Odbayar and Atsushi Fujii

17:30–18:00 *Translations of Ambiguous Hindi Pronouns to Possible Bengali Pronouns*
Sanjay Chatterji, Sudeshna Sarkar and Anupam Basu

Korean NLP2RDF Resources

YoungGyun Hahm[1] *KyungtaeLim*[1] *YoonYongun*[2]
Jungyeul Park[3] *Key − Sun Choi*[1,2]
(1) Division of Web Science and Technology, KAIST, Daejeon, South Korea
(2) Departmentt of Computer Science, KAIST, Daejeon, South Korea
(3) Les Editions an Amzer Vak, Lannion, France
[1,2]{hahmyg, kyungtaelim, yoon, kschoi}@kaist.ac.kr [3]park@amzer-vak.fr

Abstract

The aim of Linked Open Data (LOD) is to improve information management and integration by enhancing accessibility to the existing various forms of open data. The goal of this paper is to make Korean resources linkable entities. By using NLP tools, which are suggested in this paper, Korean texts are converted to RDF resources and they can be connected with other RDF triples. It is worth noticing that to the best of our knowledge there is a few of publicy available Korean NLP tools. For this reason, the Korean NLP platform presented here will be available as open source. And it is shown in this paper that the result of this NLP platform can be used as Linked Data entities.

Keywords: Korean Natural Language Processing, NLP2RDF, Linked Open Data.

1 Introduction

Research on Linked Open Data (LOD)[1] on the Web is relatively new, but it is rapidly growing nowadays. The aim of LOD is to improve information management and integration by enhancing accessibility to the existing various formats of open data. To ease the integration of data from different sources, it is desirable to use standards (Bizer et al., 2009) such as the W3C Resource Description Framework (RDF).

There is a huge amount of unstructured text in many languages in web pages. Traditionally, these web pages have been interlinked using *hyperlinks*. However, researchers in the domain of the semantic web are focusing on data and resources, rather than web pages. In the context of semantic web, such resources are usually modelled as RDF triples (Bauer and Kaltenböck, 2011).

This paper aims to describe an NLP platform presented in (Rezk et al., 2012), but focuses on the Korean language processing. Such detailed desciption was missing in (Rezk et al., 2012). In (Rezk et al., 2012) the authors present a novel framework to acquire entities from unstructured Korean text and describe them as RDF resoruces. The main contributions of this paper are as follows: *(1)* Describing in detail how to build an open Korean NLP platform which produces POS tag, CFG and DG parsing results from one-time input; and *(2)* Providing further details on how to convert NLP outputs to the RDF. The goals of this converting are to achieve universal interoperability between the results of several NLP tools, and make Korean resource to linkable entities.

Existing Korean NLP tools, such as a morphological analyser and a syntactic parser, are reused and merged. The Sejong corpus and its POS tagset (Korean Language Institue, 2012) are used as training data. In this case the output provides RDF so entities which tokenized morpheme units have an identifier URI and can be link with existing RDF stores from the LOD-cloud. Especially, entities can be mapped with subjects in DBpedia triples.

Section 2 surveys previous work on Korean NLP and linked data. The Korean NLP platform is described with a more detailed explanation in section 3. Section 4 provides some new details on how to convert the NLP output to RDF and how to link entities with Wikipedia pages, and some tries to link entities with Wikipedia page. We discuss a conclusion in Section 5.

2 Related Work

A prime example of an NLP platform which put out RDF outputs for linked data is Stanford Core-NLP[2]. Stanford Core-NLP puts out various NLP analysis results like POS tagging, CFG parsing, DG parsing and so on for one-time input. And, by using wrapper[3] which implemented by the NLP2RDF[4] project team, those results are converted to RDF in compliance with NIF.

Actually, sharing results in Korean NLP fields is still in its early stage. Researches on Korean parsers have been focused on DG parsing *e.g.* (Chung, 2004) because Korean word order is relatively free compared to other languages. Phrase-structured Sejong Treebank is transformed into the form of DG in (Choi and Palmer, 2011). Research for CFG parsing by using Sejong Treebank has progressed (Choi et al., 2012), but it is not active and disclosure of its research results and it also true that the lack of interoperability because a variety of tools put out different format results.

In English the minimal unit for parsing is a word, but, in Korean, eojeol is a basic space unit

[1] `http://lod2.eu`
[2] `http://nlp.stanford.edu/software/corenlp.shtml`
[3] `http://nlp2rdf.org/implementations/stanford-corenlp`
[4] `http://nlp2rdf.org`

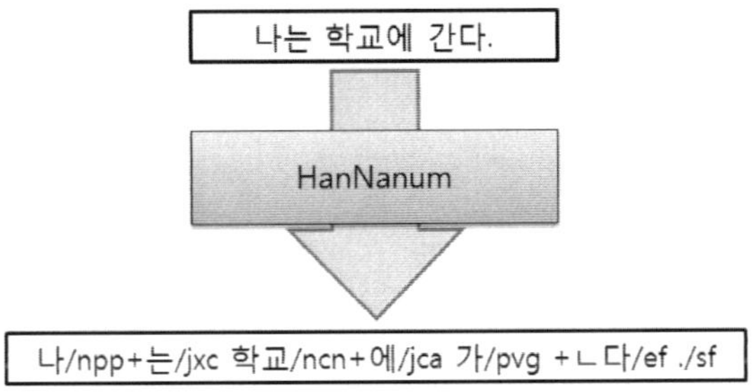

Figure 1: An example morpheme analysing Korean sentences by using HanNanum

which separated from another eojeol with white-space. An eojeol is a word or its variant word form agglutinated with grammatical affixes, and eojeols are separated by white space as in English written texts (Choi et al., 2011). Each morpheme is represented by its own POS tag so the morphological analyser is required as pre-processing for the parser. There are some existing researches about that issue and a few tools are opened already such as HanNanum (Park et al., 2010).

Research for Link Discovery issue is still on-going and there are some results such as LIMES[5] and DBpedia Spotlight[6]. Out research, such as the study of flows, attempts to outline an alternative reading of the link discovery issue. Inspiring entities are converted to RDF triples which have an URI by using our NLP platform; there are also some attempts to make links for these triples with Wikipedia page.

3 Korean Natural Language Processing Platform

Various results formats from NLP tools cause obstructive problems. So there are needs to implement one platform get one-time input. This paper describes efforts to make Korean NLP platform, and make them available as open sources. An existing morphological analyser and a syntactic parser are used and integrated in this way. Since some deficiency has been brought up, further improvement will be conducted.

And the goal of this NLP platform in this paper is that extracting entities and finding the relation between each entity from Korean resources. Morphological analyser and parser is used for this work. Details are explained in follow subsections and section 4.

3.1 Morphological Analyser

The Korean parser presented in section 3.2 requires morphologically tokenized sentences as its input. For example, English words separated by whitespace are minimal analysis units. A Korean space unit eojeol is combined with multiple morphemes. So, morphological analyser is required for splitting these morhemes from eojeol. There are two reasons: 1) most parsers consider a word which are separated by white-space as the unit of parsing. 2) For our goal, acquiring entities from Korean text. By this work, noun-tagged words can be splitted with grammatical affixes so that each word can be entities which some stacks of LOD-cloud.

As an element of Korean NLP2RDF resources, a morphological analyser, HanNanum[7] developed

[5] `http://aksw.org/projects/limes`
[6] `http://dbpedia.org/spotlight`
[7] `http://sourceforge.net/projects/hannanum`

```
Java –jar Berkeleyparser_korV2.jar "나는 학교에 간다."

(ROOT
        (S (NP_SBJ (NP 나) (JX 는))
          (VP (NP_AJT (NNG 학교) (JKB 에))
             (VP (VV가) (EF ㄴ다) (SF .)))))
```

Figure 2: An example phrese structured output

```
"나는 학교에 간다."

1. 나/NP+ 는/JX                 3        NP_SBJ
2. 학교/NNG + 에/JKB            3        NP_AJT
3. 가/VV + ㄴ다/EF + ./SF       0        VP        ROOT
```

Figure 3: An example DG results

by KAIST Semantic Web Research Center[8] is employed. HanNanum was developed in C in 1999, and re-implemented in Java in 2010. It is an NLP tool which can be used independently, and include a POS tagger. HanNanum is divided into three parts depending on the level of analysis.

1. Pre-processing: Sentence boundary recognition, filtering, auto-spacing and stemming.
2. Morphological Analysis: Generate all possible morphological analysis results from each eojeol.
3. POS tagging: Assign POS tags by selecting the most probabilistic results.

HanNanum has two problems as a morphological analyser: 1) dated dictionary, 2) excessive analysis for *josa* ('postpostion'). The dated dictionary causes a lot of unknown words and might assign wrong POS tags. It amplifies eventual parsing errors. Too finely analysed josa can reate unnecessary ambiguities.

3.2 Phrase structure parser

(Choi et al., 2012) experiments with existing parsers (Stanford, Berkeley and Bikel) using the Sejong Treebank, and found out that the Berkeley parser yields the best performance. For this work, pre-processing and transforming Sejong Treebank research go on in a parallel way. Morphological analysis results from HanNanum are used as input to Korean Berkeley parser. Resource for HanNanum and the Korean Berkeley parser is open and available at the web page[9] . Specially, input system is modified for user convenience. Figure 2 shows input and phrase structured output of Korean Berkeley parser, and converted into DG results is shown Figure 3.

3.3 DG parser

There is no available Korean corpora which DG parsing can be trained. For this reason, using algorithms from (Choi, 2010), we develop a tool which converts CFG parsing results to the DG

[8]http://semanticweb.kaist.ac.kr

[9]http://semanticweb.kaist.ac.kr/home/index.php/KoreanParser

format. Our Korean NLP platform can return DG results from the CFG result. For example, Figure 3 "나/NP+는/JX" is an NP_SBJ (subject noun phrase) and dependent on "3. 가/VV+s다/EF+./SF" Our overall performance is about 72% on F1-score and it remains future work to improve performance. DG parser results show the relation between each entity in Korean texts.

4 Converting NLP outputs to RDF

Meaning of natural language processing results by converting to RDF is two-fold: 1) Universal Interoperability can be ensured, and 2) entities which be acquired from NLP tools can be linkable with LOD-cloud. This work can be able by using string URI in RDF and details are elaborate in 4.1.2.

The Korean NLP result format is different from NLP tool result format for other languages with the point of view in structure and vocabulary. To solve this heterogeneity problem, RDF is used to describe meta-data. It could be the basis of interoperability for NLP tools.

Also, for the semantic web, efforts to link RDF triples with the LOD-cloud are explained in this paper, by converting data from the web to RDF. Entities with *document level* URI can be linked with DBpedia entities with *conceptual level* URI.

4.1 Universal Interoperability

This section summarizes the NLP2RDF system presented in (Rezk et al., 2012). We focus on the methodology of the system to describe its resources. The results of the NLP tools depend on the used POS tag set, training set and their applications. To resolve this heterogeneity, discussion for NIF (Hellmann et al., 2012; Rizzo et al., 2012) is underway in NLP2RDF as a sub-project of LOD2. NIF suggests a standard for several different NLP outputs. Korean NLP results are also different from other NLP application results based on other languages. So these metadata (for the results of NLP tools) are described by using interoperable RDF. Ontology for Korean POS tags is defined, and the whole process is complying with the specifications of NIF. The results from Section 3 are converted to RDF triples.

4.1.1 Ontology for Korean Linguistic Annotations

The Ontologies of Linguistic Annotation (OLiA) (Chiarcos, 2012) are used to describe POS tags, which are different between languages. In Korean, the Sejong POS tagset and the KAIST POS tagset (Choi et al., 1994) are used for POS tagging. OLiA are offering an annotation model for Penn tag set[10] which is mainly used in English.

In the Penn tagset annotation model, POS tag information is the subpart structure of Linguistic Annotation domain. And OLiA are offering linking model also which is mapped between Penn annotation model and OLiA reference model. In this linking model, OLiA information is the subpart structure of Linguistic Concept domain and it is mapped with the POS tag set information. We made Sejong tagset anotation model and linking model which mapped into OLiA reference model for universal interoperability. And this models are posted at webpage[11]. Figure 4 shows the correspondence between Sejong POS tags and concepts in the OLiA reference model. The KAIST POS tagset will be also interoperable in our future work.

[10] `http://nachhalt.sfb632.uni-potsdam.de/owl/penn.owl`
[11] `http://semanticweb.kaist.ac.kr/nlp2rdf/resource/`

Tag		Sejong	OLiA
Super class		*LinguisticAnnotation/Tag/*	*LinguisticConcept/MorphosyntacticCategory/*
Adverb	MAJ	Adverb/ConjunctiveAdverb	Adverb and Conjunction/CoordinationgConjunction
	MAG	Adverb/GeneralAdverb	Adverb
Noun	NNB, NNG	Noun/CommonNoun	Noun/CommonNoun
	NNP	Noun/ProperNoun	Noun/ProperNoun
	NA, NF	Noun/LikelyNoun	Noun
NP		Pronoun	PronounOrDeterminer/Pronoun
Verb	VA	Verb/Adjective	Adjective/PredicativeAdjective
	VX	Verb/AuxiliaryPredicate	Verb/AuxiliaryVerb
	VC, VCN, VCP	Verb/Copula	Verb
	VV	Verb/VerbalPredicate	Verb
	NV	Verb	Verb
SN, XN		CardinalNumber	Quantifier/Numeral
MM		Determiner	PronounOrDeterminer/Determiner
SH, SL		ForeignWord	Residual/Foreign
IC		Interjection	Interjection
SE, SF, SO, SP, SS		Symbol	Punctuation
superclass		*LinguisticAnnotation/Tag/*	*MorphologicalCategory/*
Particle	JC, JX	Particle/AuxiliaryPostpositi on	Morpheme/MorphologicalParticle
	JKB, JKC, JKG, JKO, JKQ, JKS, JKV	Particle/CaseMarker	Morpheme/MorphologicalParticle
	XPN	Particle/Prefix	Morpheme/MorphologicalParticle/prefix
	XSA, XSN, XSV	Particle/Suffix	Morpheme/MorphologicalParticle/suffix
	EC, EF, EP, ETM, ETN	Particle/VerbalEnding	Morpheme/MorphologicalParticle/suffix
	XR	Particle/Radical *(Mapping with LikelyNoun)*	Morpheme

Figure 4: Correspondence between Sejong tags and concepts in OLiA

4.1.2 String URI

The advantage of specifying URIs for each entity (results of NLP) is two-fold: 1) entities can be described with RDF, and 2) entities can be linked-able with other RDF triples. Our goal is not only focusing on getting universal interoperability for NLP output, but also making links with LOD-cloud for Korean resources from the text. Therefore, specifying an URI for each entity is an important task.

Each noun is a morpheme unit, so URIs specification works on morpheme units. Recognized entities by morphological analysing are URI specified so that it is used as 'Subject' in RDF triples. And morpheme unit entities, especially nouns, can be used as some stacks for LOD-cloud. This will be explained in Section 4.2.

NIF provides two URI schemes: The offset and context-hash based schemes. The Hash-based URI is used for our Korean NLP platform results.

Figure 5 shows an example about URI specification for Korean word.

"나는 학교에 간다" (I go to school)

'학교' (school)
Hash_15_2_c3508b1509ed7789297de77cfd9fb14f_학교

Figure 5: An example URI specification for Korean word

4.2 Linking Korean Resources with the LOD-cloud

Each of the morphemes obtained by NLP tools appears in RDF as entities with a POS tag and an URI. Actually this URI is at *document level*. Entities which appear in sentences have limited meaning in a sentence, document, text, or web page, and the described RDF information is just POS and grammatical role. These entities are isolated and restrictive.

Producing RDF from NLP results makes entities get an URI so they can be linkable. With these URIs we can link entities with RDF resources LOD-cloud, for example, DBpedia. We assume that entities of DBpedia have *conceptual level* URI and reliable information enough as a collective intelligence.

Our goal is to link Korean resources converted to RDF by NLP tools to stacks of the LOD-cloud. For example, some system can show the grammatical role of entities and DBpedia triple information. First step for this goal is to make links for entities to the Korean Wikipedia pages. The purpose of this work is the first step in the progress of experimenting Link Discovery for Korean. Our approach first accesses NLP results which obtains all nouns. We then query the Noun class using the data property anchor of to get the string. System checks the Wikipedia page for such a string. If a page exists, a link is created for the Wikipedia page. That is why we use a Wikipedia page because DBpedia always shows always page even there are no information for strings.

This system has been implemented on the web site (Semantic Web Research Center, 2012), available to anyone. This web site provides the following two functions: 1) Return a variety NLP results such as morpological analysing, CFG and DG parsing from one input text; 2) Make Links to Korea Wikipedia pages for each entity which noun-tagged words.

Here on link discovery of Korean resource, two issues are still remaining:

1. Efficient algorithms for approaches to DBpedia.
2. Using synonym relations.

Our current link discovery method is just string matching with Levenshtein distance. This method is simple; there are many limitations to finding links this way. As many other approaches such as LIMES, we need to develop efficient and adequate an algorithm for Korean.

Using synonym relations can be an alternative way to extend the capabilities of the link discovery approach. CoreNet (Choi, 2003) will be considered as pertinent resources for this issue.

5 Conclusion and Future Work

The focus of this study is two-fold: First, we developed the Korean NLP platform which returns a variety of NLP result outputs from one-time input, and make it publicly available. However, further improvement for Korean NLP tools is required for Link discovery. In particular the morpheme analyser should be modified. Second, we provided further details on how results of NLP tools are mapped into RDF. It is worth noticing that the RDF triples generated in this framework follow the NIF standard. In particular, the Sejong tagset linking model is built and used for universal interoperability for Korean NLP. Moreover, resolving the link discovery issue will be our future work.

Acknowledgement

This research was supported by the Industrial Technology International Cooperation Program (FT-1102, Creating Knowledge out of Interlinked Data) of MKE/KIAT.

References

Bauer, F. and Kaltenböck, M. (2011). *Linked Open Data: The Essentials.* Edition mono/monochrom, Vienna.

Bizer, C., Heath, T., and Berners-Lee, T. (2009). Linked data - the story so far. *Journal on Semantic Web and Information Systems (IJSWIS); Special Issue on Linked Data*, 5(3):1–22.

Chiarcos, C. (2012). Ontologies of linguistic annotation: Survey and perspectives. In Chair), N. C. C., Choukri, K., Declerck, T., Doğan, M. U., Maegaard, B., Mariani, J., Odijk, J., and Piperidis, S., editors, *Proceedings of the Eight International Conference on Language Resources and Evaluation (LREC'12)*, Istanbul, Turkey. European Language Resources Association (ELRA).

Choi, D., Park, J., and Choi, K.-S. (2012). Korean treebank transformation for parser training. In *Proceedings of the ACL 2012 Joint Workshop on Statistical Parsing and Semantic Processing of Morphologically Rich Languages*, pages 78–88, Jeju, Republic of Korea. Association for Computational Linguistics.

Choi, J. D. and Palmer, M. (2011). Statistical dependency parsing in korean: From corpus generation to automatic parsing. In *Proceedings of the Second Workshop on Statistical Parsing of Morphologically Rich Languages*, pages 1–11, Dublin, Ireland. Association for Computational Linguistics.

Choi, K.-S. (2003). CoreNet: Chinese-japanese-korean wordnet with shared semantic hierarchy. In *Proceedings of Natural Language Processing and Knowledge Engineering*, pages 767–770.

Choi, K.-S., Han, Y. S., Han, Y. G., and Kwon, O. W. (1994). Kaist tree bank project for korean: Present and future development. In *Proceedings of the International Workshop on Sharable Natural Language Resources*, pages 7–14.

Choi, K.-S., Isahara, H., and Sun, M. (2011). *Language resource management - Word segmentation of written texts - Part 2: Word segmentation for Chinese, Japanese and Korean*, ISO 24614-2.

Choi, Jinho D.; Palmer, M. (2010). Robust constituent-to-dependency conversion for english. In *Proceedings of the 9th International Workshop on Treebanks and Linguistic Theories (TLT'9)*, pages 55–66, Tartu, Estonia.

Chung, H. (2004). *Statistical Korean Dependency Parsing Model based on the Surface Contextual Information*. PhD thesis, Korea University.

Hellmann, S., Lehmann, J., and Auer, S. (2012). Linked-data aware uri schemes for referencing text fragments. In *Proceedings of the 18th International Conference on Knowledge Engineering and Knowledge Management (EKAW2012)*, Galway City, Ireland.

Park, S., Choi, D., Kim, E., and Choi, K.-S. (2010). A plug-in component-based korean morphological analyzer. In *Proceedings of HCLT2010*, pages 197–201.

Rezk, M., Park, J., Yoon, Y., Lim, K., Larsen, J., Hahm, Y., and Choi, K.-S. (2012). Korean Linked Data on the Web: From Text to RDF. In *Proceedings of JIST2012:Joint International Semantic Technology Conference*, Nara, Japan.

Rizzo, G., Troncy, R., Hellmann, S., and Bruemmer, M. (2012). NERD meets NIF: Lifting NLP extraction results to the linked data cloud. In *LDOW 2012, 5th Workshop on Linked Data on the Web, April 16, 2012, Lyon, France*, Lyon, FRANCE.

Semantic Web Research Center (2012). Korean NLP2RDF demo site, `http://semanticweb.kaist.ac.kr/nlp2rdf`, KAIST.

Building Large Scale Text Corpus for Tibetan Natural Language Processing by Extracting Text from Web Pages

Huidan LIU[1,2] *Minghua NUO*[1,2] *Jian WU*[1] *Yeping HE*[1]
(1) Institute of Software, Chinese Academy of Sciences, Beijing, China, 100190
(2) University of Chinese Academy of Sciences, Beijing, China, 100190
{huidan,minghua,wujian,yeping}@iscas.ac.cn

Abstract

In this paper, we propose an approach to build a large scale text corpus for Tibetan natural language processing. We find the distribution of Tibetan web pages on the internet with a crawler which can identify whether or not a web page contains Tibetan text. Three biggest web sites are selected, and topic pages are selected with a rule based method by checking the url. The layout structures of selected pages are analysed, and topic related information are extracted based on web site specific rules. Consequently, we get a corpus including more than 65 thousands documents, nearly 1.59 million sentences or 35 million syllables in total.

Title and Abstract in Chinese

抽取网页文本为藏文自然语言处理构建大规模文本语料库

在本文中，我们提出了一种为藏文自然语言处理构建大规模文本语料库的方法。我们首先使用网络爬虫技术，并结合藏文网页的编码识别技术判断一个网页中是否包含藏文文本，并据此考察互联网上藏文网页的分布情况。然后，我们选择了三个最大的藏文网站，根据网页的 URL，利用预先定义的规则，判断网页是 Hub 页面还是 Topic 页面。之后，我们分析了每个网站的 Topic 页面的布局结构特点，并利用正则表达式编制了相应的 Topic 相关文本的抽取规则。采用上述方法，我们构建了一个包含 6.5 万文档，共计 159 万句、3500 万藏文音节字的文本语料库。

Keywords: Tibetan, text corpus, web page, crawler, information extraction .

Keywords in Chinese: 藏文, 文本语料, 网页, 爬虫, 信息抽取.

1 Introduction

Text corpora are the basis of natural language processing. But text corpora for Tibetan are seldom reported. It's an urgent task to build text corpora for Tibetan. As the web is a large data source, we have been seeking methods to get text from the web to build a large scale Tibetan text corpus. This paper reports the work.

The paper is organized as follows: In Section 2 we recall related work on Tibetan corpora and web as corpus for other language. In Section 3, we describe our research on the distribution of Tibetan web pages, then propose the strategy and methods to select web sites, get web pages and extract text from them. We introduce the corpus in Section 4 and then concludes the paper.

2 Related work

We review the work related to Tibetan corpora in this section. As we are reporting our work on getting corpus from the web, we also review the work on "web as corpus".

2.1 Reported Tibetan text corpora

Currently, the reported Tibetan corpora are all task-oriented, mainly for word segmentation and POS tagging. Chen et al. (2003a,b) built a corpus including 500 sentences (5890 words) as the test set. Caizhijie (2009a,b) also built a corpus including about 800 Kb text. Sun et al. (2009, 2010) used a corpus including 435 sentences (4067 words) as the test set in their research. These corpora are all for word segmentation. Norbu et al. (2010) described the initial effort in segmenting the Dzongkha (Tibetan) scripts. Their experiments are made on 8 corpora in different domains, which include only 714 words in total. Chungku et al. (2010) described the Dzongkha corpus for part-of-speech tagging and proposed a tag set containing 66 tags which is applied to annotate their corpus. The corpus contains 570247 tokens in 7 domains.

From the merely reports, we find that not only the number of corpora but also the scales of them are both very small, which shows that Tibetan text corpora are far from enough.

2.2 Web as corpus

In recent years, as the internet grows rapidly, it's already an over large data source and has been increasingly used as a source of linguistic data (Kilgarriff and Grefenstette, 2003). Many researchers has begin to building corpora with web text. Boleda et al. (2006); Zuraw (2006); Guevara (2010); Dickinson et al. (2010) presented the monolingual corpora for Catalan, Tagalog, Norwegian and Korean respectively which are built by crawling the web. Resnik (1998, 1999) developed "STRAND" while Chen and Nie (2000) also developed "PTMiner" to mining parallel bilingual text from the web. We are inspired by those work to build a large scale text corpus for Tibetan natural language processing.

But web pages are semi-structured data, it's a problem how to extract only topic related text. Cai et al. (2003) presents an automatic top-down, tag-tree independent approach to detect web content structure. In this paper, we will adopt the idea to analyse the layout structure of the web page, but use more simple rules to extract text.

3 Distribution of Tibetan web pages on the internet

We use a crawler with a seed url list including a certain Tibetan web sites. Then, with a Tibetan web page examiner, the crawler checks each fetched web page whether or not there is some Tibetan text in it. If Tibetan text is found in the page, then urls of all pages it links to will be append to the fetching list. This procedure continues until the fetching list is empty, which means that there is no new Tibetan web pages are found. The procedure is also described in Figure 1.

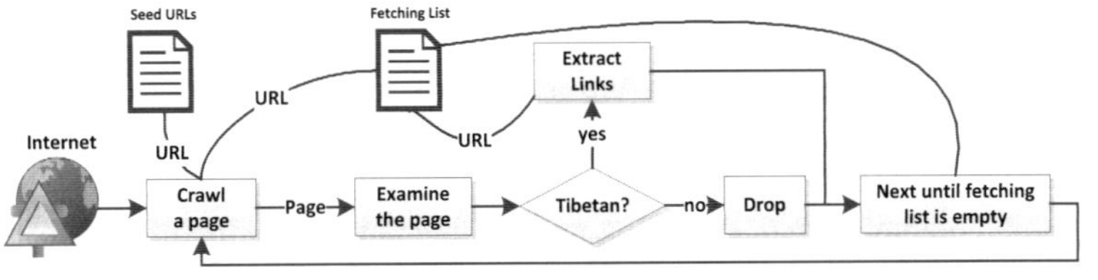

Figure 1: The procedure of finding Tibetan web pages.

Implementing this method, we build a Tibetan web text mining system. It starts to run on January 12 in 2011, and keeps running until now. Data are collected on April 13 in 2012. It's shown that the mining system find 150 Tibetan web sites and more than 130000 web pages after deduplication. Table 1 shows the web page numbers of the biggest 10 web sites.

Order	URL	♯page	(%)	accumulative ♯page	accumulative (%)
1	http://tb.chinatibetnews.com	18,160	13.79%	18,160	13.79%
2	http://tibet.people.com.cn	12,343	9.37%	30,503	23.16%
3	http://ti.tibet3.com	11,923	9.05%	42,426	32.21%
4	http://tb.tibet.cn	9,177	6.97%	51,603	39.17%
5	http://tibet.cpc.people.com.cn	6,251	4.75%	57,854	43.92%
6	http://blog.nbyzwhzx.com	4,203	3.19%	62,057	47.11%
7	http://blog.himalayabon.com	3,786	2.87%	65,843	49.98%
8	http://www.qhtb.cn	3,574	2.71%	69,417	52.70%
9	http://www.tibetcm.com	3,462	2.63%	72,879	55.32%
10	http://ti.gzznews.com	3,358	2.55%	76,237	57.87%

Table 1: Page numbers of the 10 biggest Tibetan web sites.

From Table 1 we see that nearly half (49.98%) of the web pages are intensively distributed in the 7 web sites, which is a plus factor for us to extract Tibetan text from web pages, because we can focus on only some biggest web sites.

4 Get Tibetan text from the web

In this section, we report the methods to select web sites, web pages and to extract text from web pages.

4.1 Selection of web sites

Because there are not so many Tibetan web sites and the web pages are intensively distributed, it's practical for us to use manually generated site specific rules to extract text one site by one site. With this idea, three biggest websites are selected. Table 2 shows information about them. As the sites are hold by newspaper offices, which have high quality standards for publishing, the quality of the corpus is guaranteed.

Order	Host URL	Site Name	Holder
1	http://tb.chinatibetnews.com	China Tibet News	Tibet Daily
2	http://tibet.people.com.cn	China Tibet Online	People's Daily
3	http://ti.tibet3.com	Tibetan's Web of China	Qinghai Daily

Table 2: Information about the selected web sites.

4.2 Selection of web pages

Web pages can be classified into two kinds, namely "topic" and "hub". A topic page contains long text in it while a hub page contains many links to the topic pages. As our target is to extract Tibetan text from the web pages. We only care about the topic pages rather than the hub pages. But in the URL list, which one is the URL of a topic page?

Site	Example URLs
China Tibet News	http://tb.chinatibetnews.com/news/2012-02/16/content_884280.htm http://tb.chinatibetnews.com/xzmeishi/2011-12/05/content_831210.htm http://tb.chinatibetnews.com/xzzongjiao/2011-10/21/content_798694.htm
China Tibet Online	http://tibet.people.com.cn/141101/15137028.html http://tibet.people.com.cn/141101/15199715.html http://tibet.people.com.cn/15143391.html
Tibetan's Web of China	http://ti.tibet3.com/economy/2011-01/14/content_370366.htm http://ti.tibet3.com/folkways/2008-12/10/content_3541.htm http://ti.tibet3.com/medicine/2009-10/27/content_99171.htm

Table 3: Example URLs of topic pages in the three sites.

Site	Example URLs
China Tibet News	http://tb.chinatibetnews.com/xzpinglun/node_698.htm http://tb.chinatibetnews.com/shehuiminsheng/index.html http://tb.chinatibetnews.com/xzcaijing/index.html
China Tibet Online	http://tibet.people.com.cn/140827/141059/index3.html http://tibet.people.com.cn/96372/125163/index.html http://tibet.people.com.cn/141101/index11.html
Tibetan's Web of China	http://ti.tibet3.com/culture/index.htm http://ti.tibet3.com/tour/node_701.htm http://ti.tibet3.com/economy/index.htm

Table 4: Example URLs of hub pages in the three sites.

Table 3 and Table 4 show some URLs of topic pages and hub pages of the three Tibetan web sites respectively. Comparing tens of thousands of URLs of the three web sites, we find the following rules:

- The topic URLs of "China Tibet News" and "Tibetan Web of China" have the pattern of "{host}/{column}/{year}-{month}/{date}/content_{articleid}.htm". Everyone of them contains the string "content_".
- The hub URLs of "China Tibet News" and "Tibetan Web of China" contain the string "index" or "node".
- The topic URLs of "China Tibet Online" have the pattern of "{host}/{columnid}/{articleid}.html". Characters between the host URL "{host}" and the file suffix name "html" are numbers or slash.
- The hub URLs of "China Tibet Online" contain the string "index".

With these rules, we make text extraction only on the topic pages, while URL extraction are made on both the hub pages and the topic pages.

4.3 Text extraction

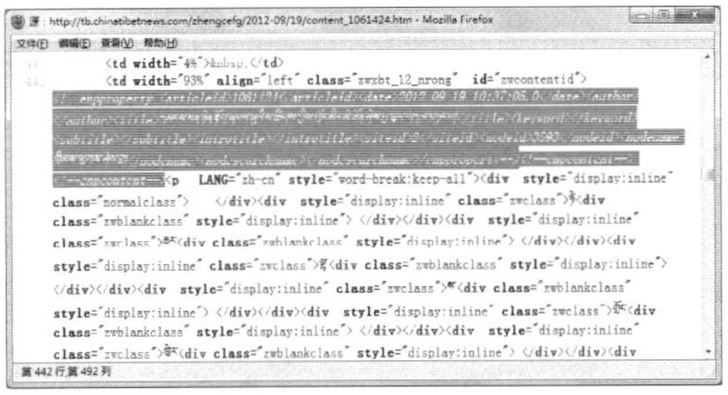

Figure 2: Commented text in a web page from "China Tibet News".

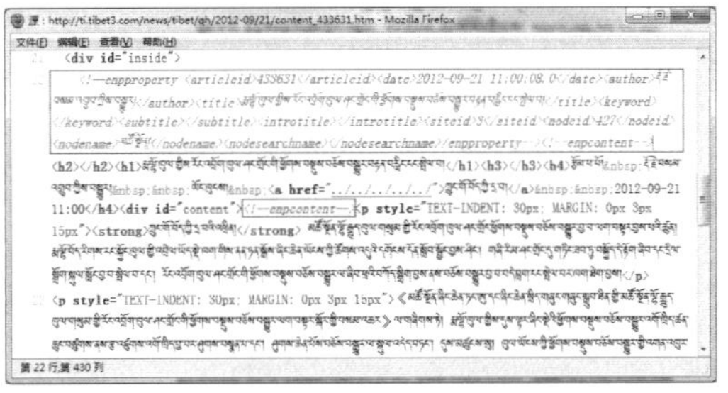

Figure 3: Commented text in a web page from "Tibetan's Web of China".

Then, we analyse each topic page to find whether there is a rule to extract topic related text. It's a surprise that we find some commented text from the html file of topic pages of "China Tibet News". Figure 2 shows the commented text in a web page[1] from "China Tibet News". The shadowed text in the figure shows many information about the page, including title, subtitle, publish date, author, and so on. Although some of the field values are kept empty, it provides us a simple method to extract those information. Unsurprisingly, the text following the shadowed text are the content of the topic, which is followed by another segment of commented text: "`<!--/enpcontent--><!--/enpcontent-->` ".

Then, we get the following rules.

- Tags and text between '<!–enpproperty>' and '/enpproperty–>' are useful information about the topic. which can be directly used as XML format text.
- HTML tags and text between the inner pair of '`<!--enpcontent-->`' and '`<!--/enpcontent-->`' are the content of the topic in HTML format.

What a big surprise! We find almost the same commented text in the topic pages from the third web site "Tibetan's Web of China". Figure 3 shows the HTML file of a web page[2] from it. But is it a coincidence? We get the information that both of the two web sites are using the same computer management system of news gathering and editing, which is a product of Beijing Founder Electronics company, to manage their articles and web pages.

We have no luck in processing pages from "China Tibet Online". But we still get a clue after analysing the structure of some web pages from this site. Figure 4 shows the structure of a web page[3] from this site. From the figure, we see that there are some HTML tags giving the boundaries of different text blocks, including:

- String '<div class="wb_p1">' indicates the start of the title, and the title is surrounded by HTML tags "<h1>" and "</h1>". The text between the following "<h2>" and "</h2>" may be the subtitle.

[1]`http://tb.chinatibetnews.com/zhengcefg/2012-09/19/content_1061424.htm`
[2]`http://ti.tibet3.com/news/tibet/qh/2012-09/21/content_433631.htm`
[3]`http://tibet.people.com.cn/15260188.html`

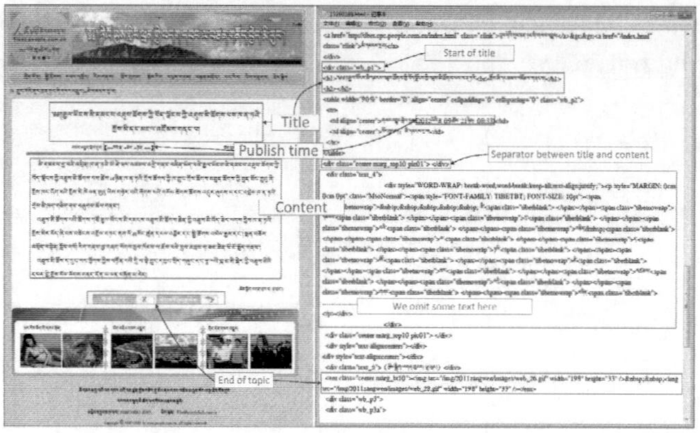

Figure 4: The structure of a web page from "China Tibet Online".

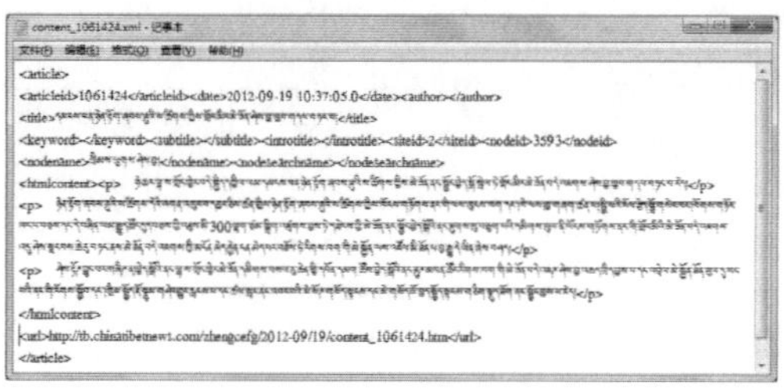

Figure 5: The text extracted from a page from "China Tibet news".

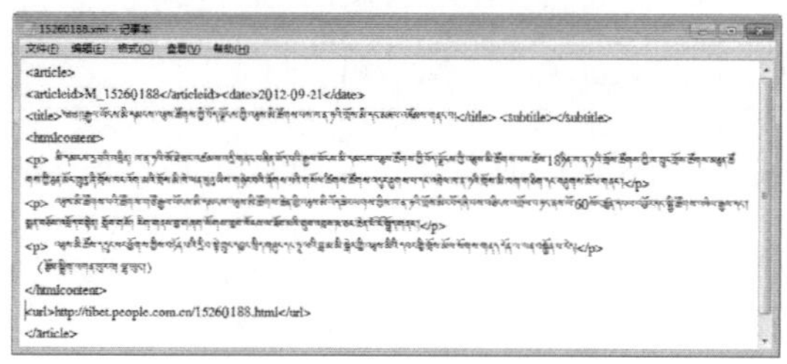

Figure 6: The text extracted from a page from "China Tibet Online".

- String '<div class="center marg_top10 pic01"> </div>' is the separator between the title block and the content block.
- String '<div class="text_4">' indicates the start of the content block.
- String '<em class="center marg_bt10">...</em>' indicates the end of the content block.

Taking advantage of the HTML tag information, we also can extract the topic related information from the web pages in the web site "China Tibet Online".

Then, we use another crawler, which is deployed with a larger link depth than the former crawler, to download web pages from the three web sites, and implement the rules mentioned above by regular expressions. Topic related text are extracted from the web pages. we filtered out most HTML tags, and convert them into XML format. Figure 5 and Figure 6 show the results.

5 The corpus

In this section, we have to introduce the counting units because Tibetan is different from many other languages. The corpus is introduced after that.

5.1 About the counting units

In Tibetan, syllables are separated by a delimiter known as "tsheg", which is simply a superscripted dot. Thus the syllable in Tibetan is a unit smaller than or equal to a word, and meanwhile it's larger than or equal to a character, just like a "hanzi" in Chinese. Figure 7 shows the structure of a Tibetan word which is made up of two syllables and means "show" or "exhibition". Another delimiter known as "shed" indicates the sentence boundary, which looks like a vertical pipe. Figure 8 shows a Tibetan sentence. In this paper, we use "sentence" and "syllable" as the units to give a more sensitive description of the scale of the corpus.

Figure 7: A Tibetan word.

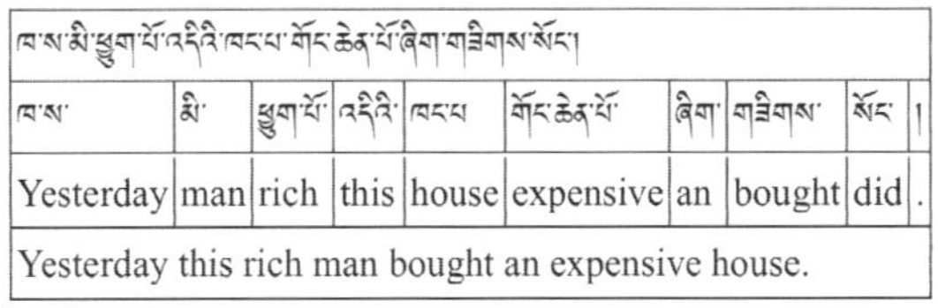

Figure 8: A Tibetan sentence.

5.2 The scale of the corpus

We get more than 65 thousands documents from the three web sites, including nearly 1.59 million sentences or 35 million syllables in total. Table 5 shows the data about the corpus. The corpus may be used to make many kinds of statistics, such as character frequencies, syllable frequencies, to train the language models. It can also be used as a basis to build corpus for other natural language processing tasks.

Order	Site Name	♯document	(%)	♯sentence	♯syllable
1	China Tibet News	31,304	47.88%	815,000	20,264,896
2	China Tibet Online	18,558	28.39%	339,096	7,595,860
3	Tibetan's Web of China	15,515	23.73%	435,623	7,182,505
Total		65,377	100.00%	1,589,719	35,043,261

Table 5: The scale of the corpus.

Note that the document numbers in Table 5 are great than those in Table 1. It results from two factors:(1) New pages are created after the data in Table 1 are collected. (2) The crawler used to extract Tibetan text corpus is deployed with a bigger link depth than the one in section 3.

5.3 Domains in the corpus

Table 3 shows some URLs from the three web sites. We find that the URL of a page from "China Tibet News" or "Tibetan's Web of China" gives the evidence that which column or sub column, and consequently which domain it belongs to. The following examples shows it.

- The url "http://tb.chinatibetnews.com/xzmeishi/2011-12/05/content_831210.htm" shows it belongs to a column called "xzmeishi". so it must be a topic page about Tibetan foods, because "xz" is the abbreviated form of Chinese word "xizang" written in Pinyin[4], which means the Tibetan Autonomous Region, while "meishi" means "delicious food".
- Another url "http://ti.tibet3.com/medicine/2009-10/27/content_99171.htm" from "Tibetan's web of China" shows it belongs to "Tibetan Medicine" domain.

[4] A Latin transliteration method for Chinese.

With this method, we classify the documents into different domains. Table 6 and Table 7 show the numbers of documents from the two web sites , in different domains. Comparing the two tables, we find that "News" shares a large part of the documents, especially for those from "Tibetan's web of China", which is up to 86.88%. Documents from "China Tibet News" are more balanced. These parts of corpus can be used for text classification.

Order	Domain	♯document	(%)	♯sentence	♯syllable
1	Art	1,277	4.08%	49,250	614,269
2	Finance & Economy	503	1.61%	9,785	268,098
3	History & Geometry	443	1.42%	8,546	151,663
4	News	10,395	33.21%	272,745	7,446,822
5	Picture	2,548	8.14%	16,935	346,175
6	Politics & Law	5,329	17.02%	181,545	4,659,379
7	Rural Life	1,238	3.95%	23,891	646,246
8	Social Life	473	1.51%	6,385	173,766
9	Special Issues	6,100	19.49%	175,173	4,561,724
10	Technology & Education	943	3.01%	24,716	600,806
11	Tibetan Buddhism	792	2.53%	22,318	352,642
12	Tibetan Food	92	0.29%	1,682	16,640
13	Tibetan Medicine	508	1.62%	10,436	155,372
14	Tour	663	2.12%	11,593	271,294
Total		31,304	100.00%	815,000	20,264,896

Table 6: Domains in the documents from "China Tibet News".

Order	Domain	♯document	(%)	♯sentence	♯syllable
1	Art	77	0.50%	2,987	47,558
2	Culture	710	4.58%	86,155	860,747
3	Economy	73	0.47%	7,143	121,440
4	Education	11	0.07%	683	14,542
5	Music	78	0.50%	2,296	31,806
6	News	13,480	86.88%	284,337	5,218,266
7	Photo	63	0.41%	2,493	38,090
8	Policy	116	0.75%	7,062	128,992
9	Politics	124	0.80%	7,668	145,206
10	Special Issues	523	3.37%	17,537	309,100
11	Tibetan Medicine	107	0.69%	11,417	173,974
12	Tour	131	0.84%	5,489	86,773
13	Video	19	0.12%	314	5,493
14	Other	3	0.02%	42	518
Total		15,515	100.00%	435,623	7,182,505

Table 7: Domains in the documents from "Tibetan's web of China".

Conclusion and perspectives

In this paper, we proposed an approach to build a large scale text corpus for Tibetan natural language processing by extracting text from three biggest web sites. Consequently, we get a corpus including more than 65 thousands documents, nearly 1.59 million sentences or 35 million syllables in total. Parts of the corpus are classified into different domains. In the following work, we will build corpora for other tasks based on the present corpus.

Acknowledgements

The research is partially supported by National Science and Technology Major Project (No.2010ZX01036-001-002, No.2010ZX01037-001-002), National Science Foundation (No.61003117, No.61202219, No.61202220), Major Science and Technology Projects in Press and Publishing (No.0610-1041BJNF2328/23, No.0610-1041BJNF2328/26), and CAS Action Plan for the Development of Western China (No.KGCX2-YW-512).

References

Boleda, G., Bott, S., Meza, R., Castillo, C., Badia, T., and López, V. (2006). Cucweb: a catalan corpus built from the web. In *Proceedings of the 2nd International Workshop on Web as Corpus*, pages 19–26. Association for Computational Linguistics.

Cai, D., Yu, S., Wen, J., and Ma, W. (2003). Vips: a visionbased page segmentation algorithm. Technical report, Microsoft Technical Report, MSR-TR-2003-79.

Caizhijie (2009a). The design of banzhida tibetan word segmentation system. In *the 12th Symposium on Chinese Minority Information Processing.*

Caizhijie (2009b). Identification of abbreviated word in tibetan word segmentation. *Journal of Chinese Information Processing*, 23(01):35–37.

Chen, J. and Nie, J.-Y. (2000). Automatic construction of parallel english-chinese corpus for cross-language information retrieval. In *Proceedings of the sixth conference on Applied natural language processing*, ANLC '00, pages 21–28, Stroudsburg, PA, USA. Association for Computational Linguistics.

Chen, Y., Li, B., and Yu, S. (2003a). The design and implementation of a tibetan word segmentation system. *Journal of Chinese Information Processing*, 17(3):15–20.

Chen, Y., Li, B., Yu, S., and Lancuoji (2003b). An automatic tibetan segmentation scheme based on case auxiliary words and continuous features. *Applied Linguistics*, 2003(01):75–82.

Chungku, C., Rabgay, J., and Faaß, G. (2010). Building nlp resources for dzongkha: A tagset and a tagged corpus. In *Proceedings of the Eighth Workshop on Asian Language Resouces*, pages 103–110, Beijing, China. Coling 2010 Organizing Committee.

Dickinson, M., Israel, R., and Lee, S.-H. (2010). Building a korean web corpus for analyzing learner language. In *Proceedings of the NAACL HLT 2010 Sixth Web as Corpus Workshop*, pages 8–16, NAACL-HLT, Los Angeles. Association for Computational Linguistics.

Guevara, E. R. (2010). Nowac: a large web-based corpus for norwegian. In *Proceedings of the NAACL HLT 2010 Sixth Web as Corpus Workshop*, pages 1–7, NAACL-HLT, Los Angeles. Association for Computational Linguistics.

Kilgarriff, A. and Grefenstette, G. (2003). Introduction to the special issue on the web as corpus. *Computational linguistics*, 29(3):333–347.

Norbu, S., Choejey, P., Dendup, T., Hussain, S., and Muaz, A. (2010). Dzongkha word segmentation. In *Proceedings of the Eighth Workshop on Asian Language Resouces*, pages 95–102, Beijing, China. Coling 2010 Organizing Committee.

Resnik, P. (1998). Parallel strands: A preliminary investigation into mining the web for bilingual text. *Machine Translation and the Information Soup*, pages 72–82.

Resnik, P. (1999). Mining the web for bilingual text. In *Proceedings of the 37th annual meeting of the Association for Computational Linguistics on Computational Linguistics*, pages 527–534. Association for Computational Linguistics.

Resnik, P. and Smith, N. A. (2003). The web as a parallel corpus. *Comput. Linguist.*, 29(3):349–380.

Sun, Y., Luosangqiangba, Yang, R., and Zhao, X. (2009). Design of a tibetan automatic segmentation scheme. In *the 12th Symposium on Chinese Minority Information Processing*.

Sun, Y., Yan, X., Zhao, X., and Yang, G. (2010). A resolution of overlapping ambiguity in tibetan word segmentation. In *Proceedings of the 3rd International Conference on Computer Science and Information Technology*, pages 222–225.

Zuraw, K. (2006). Using the web as a phonological corpus: a case study from tagalog. In *Proceedings of the 2nd International Workshop on Web as Corpus*, pages 59–66. Association for Computational Linguistics.

A Structured Approach for Building Assamese Corpus: Insights, Applications and Challenges

Prof. Shikhar Kr. Sarma[1] *Himadri Bharali*[1] *Ambeswar Gogoi*[1] *Ratul Ch. Deka*[1] *Anup Kr. Barman*[1]
(1) DEPT. OF IT, GAUHATI UNIVERSITY, Guwahati – 781014, India
sks001@gmail.com, himadri0001@gmail.com, ambeswar@gmail.com, rdeka8258@gmail.com, anupbarman.gu@gmail.com

ABSTRACT

To study about various naturally occurring phenomenons on natural language text, a well structured text corpus is very much essential. The quality and structure of a corpus can directly influence on performance of various Natural Language Processing applications. Assamese is one of the major Indian languages used by the people of north east India. Language technology development works in Assamese language have been started at various levels, and research and development works started demanding a structured and well covered Assamese Corpus in UNICODE format. Here we present various issues and problems related to building an Assamese text corpus. We review our experience with constructing one such corpus including about 1.5 million words of Assamese language. It will provide a significant effort by serving as an important research tool for language and NLP researchers.

KEYWORDS: Assamese, Corpus, linguistics, Natural Language Processing.

1 Introduction

Language corpora are extensively used in language technology and linguistic researches. There arose a tremendous interest in building and developing computerized language corpora in recent few years. The study of digital corpora of various languages offers the students and the researchers an opportunity to work with language data with variety of tools and techniques in terms of computational procedures and programs.

Assamese is one of India's national languages and belongs to the Indo-Aryan language Family. It is spoken by about 15 million people. The matter of fact is that Assamese lacks computational linguistic resources. There are no prior computational works on this language, spoken widely in north-east India. Recently, researchers have begun to involve in the development and enrichment of the language of Assamese in the field of Natural Language Processing (NLP). Such NLP activities demanded the need of building up a large amount of corpora in the languages.

The term 'corpus' is used to refer to a collection of linguistic data (covering spoken and written) in a language for some specific purposes and these data are to be stored, managed and analysed in digital format. A corpus may be quite small, for instance, consisting of 50,000 words or texts, or very large, consisting of millions of words. The Cambridge International Corpus collected by Cambridge University Press contains 700 million words or text and it has being increased all the time. The Brown Corpus, the first computer based corpus, comprising one million words of edited written American English, was created at Brown University in early sixties. Corpus is assumed to be a representative of a given language so as to make it useful for linguistic analysis. The word 'corpus' is derived from Latin meaning 'body'. Theoretically, corpus is (C)apable (O)f (R)epresenting (P)otentially (U)nlimited (S)elections of texts.[1]

Corpus is the basis of all kinds of linguistic researches. The scope of corpus is a vast one. The areas of corpus-based researches are – grammatical studies of specific linguistic construction, building of reference grammar, lexicography, language variation and dialectology, historical linguistics, translation studies, language acquisition, language pedagogy, and natural language processing and so on.

The need of language corpora has given rise to the study of corpus linguistics. It is not a branch in linguistics, but a methodology which helps in pursuing linguistic research. From the very beginning, modern corpus linguistics has been closely associated with the development of computer software for corpus analysis. In modern corpus linguistics, the linguists and the computer scientists share a common goal that it is important to depend on the real or actual language data (speech or written) for carrying out any kind of linguistic analysis. Moreover, it is an approach which satisfies two main purposes: how people use language in day-to-day communication and to build up intelligent system to interact with human beings.

2 Related Study

Modern day corpora are of various types. In fact, it is a very crucial task of classifying language corpora into different types. However, written corpus, spoken corpus, general corpus, monolingual corpus, bilingual corpus, un-annotated corpus, annotated corpus, parallel and learner corpus are worth mentioning.

India is a land of diverse linguistic groups. But in comparison to other advanced countries, it possesses no language corpora due to the lack of language technology development. All the linguistic researches are done in traditional mode. But recently it has made a deliberate attempt to build digital language corpus. Generation of corpora could enhance various linguistic and NLP developments and thus protect languages from extinction.

The Kolhapur corpus of Indian Languages, created at the Shivaji University, Kolhapur in 1988. It consists of approximately one million words of Indian English data. But it fails to represent Indian national language used in the country.

The urge to build corpora in Indian languages is fueled by the all round growth of language technology in India. Consequently, the Department of Electronics (DOE), Govt. of India begun corpus development from 1991. The technology development for Indian languages (TDIL) programme had taken initiation in building machine-readable corpora of nearly 10 million words within three years for all Indian national languages. Indian Institute of Technology (IIT), Kanpur was entrusted to develop tool for language processing and machine-aided translation system from English to Indian languages. However, the Department of Electronics (DOE) could develop corpora of 3 million words for each Indian language and had to suspend further continuation by the end of 1994.

Later on some Indian experts had decided to start more corpus generation and processing. The Ministry of Information Technology (MIT), Govt. of India, Department of Information Technology (DIT), the Central Institute of Indian Languages (CIIL), Mysore had taken steps to create corpora in major Indian languages (Hindi, Nepali, Marathi, Konkini, Assamese, Manipuri, Kannada, Sanskrit, Bangla, Telegu, Tamil, Gujrati, Oriya, Punjabi, Malayalam, Urdu, Kashmiri). These corpora are in UNICODE and annotated according to the Corpus Encoding Standard (CES) guidelines.

---

[1] Dash, N.S. (2005) Corpus Linguistics and Language Technology: With Reference to Indian Languages, New Delhi, Mittal Publication

3 Text Corpus Generation In Assamese

In the present study, we mainly deal with the building the structure of Assamese un-annotated raw corpus comprising approximately 1.5 million words (total 1,577,750 words) and also try to highlight the problems faced during the process of building it. This huge collection of texts would be helpful in the linguistic and non-linguistic studies, cross-linguistic comparisons and, all other areas of language technologies.

There are various issues that are associated with the design, development and management of corpus. Such issues vary according to the type and utility of the corpus. In fact, speech corpus development is different from text corpus. Developing a text corpus in Assamese is concerned with the issues like the overall size or length of corpus, selection of the type of genres, the number of text and range of writers, data collection, computerizing the data and validation of raw corpus. These are discussed below:

1. The overall size or length of the corpus

Size or length of corpus is an important factor of consideration. The overall size of Assamese corpus is determined as 1.5 million words (total 1,577,750 words). But before determining the length of the corpus, certain decisions are taken such as – availability of resources, time for data collection and computerizing them. So far as time factor is concerned, the present corpus is expected to be completed within approximately two years. The matter of fact is that the length of a corpus is determined not by focusing on the overall length of the corpus, but focusing more on the internal structure of the corpus: the number of genres is to be included in the corpus, the length and number of individual text samples. The expected words would be collected from three main categories: Media, learned material and literature. These main categories are again divided into some sub-categories. And accordingly, the collection of the total 1.5 million words is shown in below table:

Main Category	Category	Sub-category	Expected words per category	Root category count
Media				637000
	Newspaper		337500	
		News		
		Sports		
		Editorials		
		Reports		
		Letter		
		Cartoon		
		Horoscope		
		Arts related news		
		Science related news		
		Cookery		
		Reviews		
		Obituaries		
		Classified ads		
		Publicity		
		Trivia		
	Magazine		299500	
		Film		
		Women's		
		Informative/General		
		Children		
		Others		
Learned Material				229250
	Science		116250	
		Biology		
		Botany		
		Computer		
		Geoscience		
		Chemistry		

		Mathematics		
		Physics		
		Medicine		
		Zoology		
		Others		
	Arts		113000	
		Economics		
		Linguistics		
		History		
		Psychology		
		Sociology		
		Law		
		Politics		
		Philosophy		
		Religion		
		Other		
Literature				711500
	Short fiction		120000	
		Light fiction		
		Sentimental fiction		
		Science fiction		
		Detective fiction		
		Serious fiction		
	Criticism		52500	
		Plays		
		Theatre		
		Novels		
		Short stories		
	Theatre		75000	
		Full length plays		
		Comedy		
		Tragedy		
		Art plays		
		Light theatre		
	Novel		300000	
		Full length novel		
		Sentimental novel		
		Science fiction		
		Detective novel		
		Historical novel		
		Art novel		
		Auto-biographical novel		
		Other light fiction		
	Trivia		15000	
		Jokes		
		Anecdotes		
		Fables		
		Current riddles		
		Proverbs		
	Art and craft		37000	
	Letter		18500	
		Administrative		

		Personal		
	Didactic material		75000	
		Encyclopaedia		
		School and college texts		
			Total	1577750

TABLE 1- Representation of the collection of 1.5 million words from various genres.

2. Selection of genres included in the corpus

Genres are selected keeping in mind the purpose and utility of a corpus. A large number of written genres are included in Assamese corpus. These genres are listed in the Table 1 and they represent the language in true sense. Importantly, in selecting the genres we do not consider the poetry since the language structure is very much flexible depending on the writer's views.

3. Determining the number of text and range of writers included in the corpus

After selecting the genres, next task is to determine how many the numbers of texts and the range of writers to be included in the corpus of Assamese. There are a huge number of texts available in the languages, but we are very selective in determining the number of texts. Similarly, in the selection of the range of authors, we give importance to both eminent authors and little-known authors. In the selection of newspaper and magazines, we are very much selective. In case learned material, we try to cover up all necessary domains (as shown in Table 1). Regarding the text selection we also consider the time factors so that we can include texts from various time periods.

4. Collecting data

Data collection is a crucial task of building a corpus. There are various ways to collect written texts for Assamese corpus such as buying printed texts, use of library (with necessary permission), photocopying and scanning the texts etc. In this context, the issue of copyright is well maintained.

5. Computerizing data

After data collection, we prepare for entering those data in an electronic format. It is a very laborious process. And most importantly these data are only typed by the native speaker of Assamese language because a non-native speaker is not familiar with the writing style of a given language.

The composer has the most important task of entering the metadata also. He has to give certain information about the text, for example, genre of the text, type of the text (report, fiction, drama, article etc.), the name of the text, the name of author and editor, name of publisher, date of publication, place of publication, the page numbers of the texts etc.

6. Validating the raw corpus

The process of validating the whole raw corpus starts just after the completion of entering the computerized data. It is done by the experts (must be a native speaker) who possesses linguistic knowledge of Assamese. Sometimes, the data compiler validates the data himself. But the cross-validation of the data is best deserved.

4 Problems Faced During the Overall Process of Building of the Corpus:

1. Problem of availability of data

In corpus building of Assamese corpus, if the composer sometimes fails to find out certain selected text material, then he can replace that selected text by another text to that corresponding author. Besides certain academic materials like engineering and medical books are not generally found written in Assamese language. In such cases, we need to replace those materials with some other related materials available in the language.

2. Linguistic problem

In computerizing the data, it is seem to face certain linguistic problem such as

- Spelling error

The compiler faces certain spelling errors in the text materials. And it is the task of the compiler to enter the correct forms of the word in computerizing the data. Some of the common spelling errors are dealt with in building Assamese corpus mentioned below: (AS: Assamese Sentence; TF: Transliterated Assamese Form; ET: English Translation)

Error: AS: সমিচীন, দূৰ্গা, পুৰস্কাৰ

TF: *samiciin, duurgaa, puraskaar*

Correct: AS: সমীচীন, দুৰ্গা, পুৰষ্কাৰ

TF: *samiiciin, durgaa, purashkaraar*

ET: suitable, goddess Durga, award

- Spelling variation

In Assamese language, there are certain words which have more than one accepted spellings. These spelling varies from text to text depending on the writer's acceptance. Sometimes the composer seems to become confused seeing spelling variation for the same word in the text materials. He has to take crucial decision in this regard of selecting different spelling forms of the same word. In Assamese texts also such kinds of spelling variations are very frequent. Depending on the frequency of the different word forms, the composer has to keep all of them in the digital files. For example:

To represent river Ganga, two accepted spellings are গংগা (gangaa: river Ganga), গঙ্গা (gangaa: river Ganga)

To represent office, two accepted spellings are কাৰ্যালয় (kaarjyaalay: office), কাৰ্য্যালয় (kaarjyaalay: office)

- Syntactic error

Syntactic errors are commonly found in Assamese texts and it is the responsibility of the compiler to write the correct forms. For example

Error: AS: মানুহজন ঘৰলৈ যাম।

TF: *maanuhjan gharaloi zaam.*

Correct: AS: মানুহজন ঘৰলৈ যাব।

TF: *maanuhjan gharaloi zaaba.*

ET: The man will go to home.

- Dialectical variation

Assamese corpus texts contain a large amount of dialect words. These words are retained as it is. For example

AS:মাকজনীয়ে কেঁচুৱাটোৰ *হেনাহতে* মৰেমৰে।

TF: *maakjaniiye kecuwator henaahate mare*

ET: The mother has deep love for her baby.

AS: '*ঐ আপা,* এইফালে আহ', মানুহজনে মাত লগালে।

ET: Hello boy, come here, the man called.

TF: 'oi aapaa, eiphaale aah,' maanuhjane maat lagaale.

- Junk characters

Junk characters are occurred profusely in the texts due to typing error. In Assamese texts too, junk characters are dealt with care. For instance

Error: AS: পূূজা, মৌৌ, আৰুু etc.

TF: puuuujaa, mouou, aaruu

Correct: AS: পূজা, মৌ, আৰু

TF: puujaa, mou, aaru

ET: worship, bee, and

- Incomplete sentence

Incomplete sentences in the texts create problem for the compiler. It is important to avoid incomplete sentences while entering the data by the compiler. Incomplete sentence found in Assamese text materials is given below:

Error: AS: ডকাইতিৰ কথা শুনি মানুহজনে …

TF: dakaatir kathaa shuni maanuhjane …

ET: hearing about the robbery the man …

Correct: AS: ডকাইতিৰ কথা শুনি মানুহজনে *উচপ খাই উঠিল*।

TF: dakaatir kathaa shuni maanuhjane *ucap khai uthil.*

ET: hearing about the robbery the man became shocked.

- Hyphenated words

Assamese possesses hyphenated word forms. But these are not uniform in all the texts. Therefore, hyphens between words are removed in Assamese texts, except reduplicated forms.

Error: AS: লাহে-লাহে, লগে-লগে

TF: laahe-laahe, lage-lage

ET: slowly, instantly

Correct: AS: লাহে লাহে, লগে লগে

TF: laahe-laahe, lage-lage

ET: slowly, instantly

- Punctuation markers

In some texts, punctuation markers like full stop, comma, dash etc. are not marked uniformly. Two or more sentences are joined together without any overt connectors. In that case, the compiler puts appropriate punctuation markers reading out the data in the texts. Some of these errors are commonly found while building Assamese corpus, such as

Error1: AS: কৌটিল্যই লিপিকাৰৰ গুণাগুণ বিচাৰ কৰি কৈছে যে লিপিকাৰে কেৱল আখৰকেইটা লিখিব জানিলেই নহ'ব।

TF: koutilyai lipikaarar gunagun bicar kari koise ze lipikaare kewal aakharkeitaa likhib janilei nahaba

ET: after examining the writer's creations Kautilya commented that it is not sufficient for the writer only to know how to write

Error2: AS: মূৰ্তিৰ কথা শেষ নহ'ল খণ্ডতে লালজীয়ে ৰুদ্ৰ মূৰ্তি ধৰিলে

TF: muurtir kathaa shekh nahal khangate laalajiiye rudra muurti dharile

ET: Murtty did not completed his speech Lalaji became raged in anger

Correct1: AS: কৌটিল্যই লিপিকাৰৰ গুণাগুণ বিচাৰ কৰি কৈছে যে, 'লিপিকাৰে কেৱল আখৰকেইটা লিখিব জানিলেই নহ'ব।'

TF: koutilyai lipikaarar gunagun bicar kari koise ze, 'lipikaare kewal aakharkeitaa likhib janilei nahaba।'

ET: After examining the writer's creations Kautilya commented that, 'it is not sufficient for the writer only to know how to write.'

Correct2: AS: মূৰ্ত্তিৰ কথা শেষ নহ'ল। খঙতে লালজীয়ে ৰুদ্ৰ মূৰ্ত্তি ধৰিলে।
TF: muurtir kathaa shekh nahal. khangate laalajiiye rudra muurti dharile
ET: Murtty did not complete his speech. Lalaji became raged in anger.

Conclusion

In this paper, we have presented a description of processes involved in creating the raw corpus in Assamese and also a discussion on the problems faced during the process. Corpus is being regarded as a multi-dimensional in nature. Corpus in Assamese opens up new avenues in the field of language technology, communication, exchange of information, language education and linguistic activities etc. In the future, it should be our great responsibility to create bigger corpora, consisting of billions of words, in our native language. Besides, steps are to be taken in annotating the raw corpus which would result in building morphological analyzer, spell checking tool, concordancer, machine translation, speech recognition etc. in the language of Assamese.

References

Bora, L.S. (2006). *Asamiya Bhasar Ruptattva*, M/s Banalata, 2006.

Goswami, G. C. (2009). Asamiya Vyakaran Pravesh, 3rd edition. Bina Library, Guwahati. 2009.

Goswami, G. C. (2004). Asamiya Vyakaranar Maulik Vicar Pravesh, 4th edition. Bina Library, Guwahati. 2009.

Aston, G (Ed. 2004) *Learning with Corpora.* Cambridge: Cambridge University press.

Jayaram, B.D and Rajyashree, S.K.: *Corpora in Indian Languages. Central Institute of Languages Manasagangotri,* Mysore 570006, India.

Jayaram, B.D. (1996). *Development of Corpora in Indian Languages: Problems and Suggested Solutions.* Paper presented at workshop of Indian Language Corpus and its applications at CIIL, Mysore.

Ganesan, M: *Tamil Corpus Generation and Text Analysis:* Annamalai University, Annamalainagar, Tamilnadu, India.

Jaimai Purev and Chimeddorj Obdayar. (2008). *Corpus Building for Mongolian Language* in Proceedings The 6th Workshop on Asian Languae Resources, 2008

Steven A. and Steven B. (2010). *The Human Language Project: building a universal corpus of the world's languages.* In Proceedings of the 48th Annual Meeting of the Association for Computational Linguistics, Uppsala, Sweden.

N.S. Dash (2005). Corpus Languistics and Language Technology with Reference to Indian languages: Mitali Publication, New Delhi.

Charles F. Mayer: English Corpus Linguistics An Introduction. Published by the press Syndicate of the University of Cambridge.

Stella E.O. Tagnin: A Multilingual Learner Corpus in Brazil. Published: Rodopi.

McEnery and Andrew Wilson: Corpus Linguistics. Published by Edinburge University press.

Michael McCarthy: Touchstone From Corpus to Course Book. Published by the syndicate of the University of Cambridge.

Kenji Imamura and Eiichiro Sumita (2002). Bilingual Corpus Cleaning Focusing on Translation Literality. In: 7th International Conference on Spoken Language Processing (ICSLP-2002).

Dash, Niladri Sekhar: Language corpora. A Mittal Publication.

Dash, Niladri Sekhar. (2004). Language corpora: Present Indian Need. In the Proceedings of the SCALLA 2004 Working Conference.

Mitchell P. Marcus, Beatrice Santorini, Mary Ann Marcinkiewicz: Building a Large Annotated Corpus of English: The Penn Treebank. Published in: Journal Computational Linguistics - Special issue on using large corpora: II.

Motaz K. Saad, Wesam Ashour. (2010) OSAC: Open Source Arabic Corpora: Published at the 6th International conference on Electrical and Computer System (EECS,10), Nov.25-26,2010, Lefke, North Cyprus.

Corpus Building of Literary Lesser Rich Language- Bodo: Insights and Challenges

Biswajit Brahma[1] *Anup Kr. Barman*[1] *Prof. Shikhar Kr. Sarma*[1] *Bhatima Boro*[1]
(1) DEPT. OF IT, GAUHATI UNIVERSITY, Guwahati - 781014, India
bswjtbrahma@gmail.com, anupbarman.gu@gmail.com,
sks001@gmail.com, borobhatima@gmail.com

ABSTRACT

Collection of natural language texts in to a machine readable format for investigating various linguistic phenomenons is call a corpus. A well structured corpus can help to know how people used that language in day-to-day life and to build an intelligent system that can understand natural language texts. Here we review our experience with building a corpus containing 1.5 million words of Bodo language. Bodo is a Sino Tibetan family language mainly spoken in Northern parts of Assam, the North Eastern state of India. We try to improve the quality of Bodo corpora considering various characteristics like representativeness, machine readability, finite size etc. Since Bodo is one of the Indian language which is lesser reach on literary and computationally we face big problem on collecting data and our generated corpus will help the researchers in both field.

KEYWORD : Bodo language, Corpus, Linguistics, Natural Language Processing.

1 Introduction

The term corpus is derived from Latin corpus "body" which it means as a representative collection of texts of a given language, dialect or other subset of a language to be used for linguistic analysis. Precisely, it refers to (a) (loosely) anybody of text; (b) (most commonly) a body of machine readable text; and (c) (more strictly) a finite collection of machine-readable texts sampled to be representative of a language or variety (Mc Enery and Wilson 1996: 218). Again, Corpus is a machine readable texts (both spoken and written) document stored in machine systematically collected from different sources. It is an important text in digital media world. It is defined as corpus and in plural corpora a collection of linguistic data, either compiled as written texts or as a transcription of recorded speech. The main purpose of a corpus is to verify a hypothesis about language - for example, to determine how the usage of a particular sound, word, or syntactic construction varies. Corpus linguistics deals with the principles and practice of using corpora in language study. A computer corpus is a large body of machine-readable texts[1]. So it is the computerization of varieties text (various domains of texts such as literature, science, sports etc.) of a given language. Corpus may be of monolingual, bilingual and multi lingual format of machine readable data etc. It is an annotated and tagged component of parts of speech. It is most important for computing to make it accessible worldwide via internet. Moreover it is a valid machine readable data of a given language which gives us proper information of a language where it follows linguistics principles.

The need of language corpora has given rise to the study of corpus linguistics. It is not a branch of linguistics but the methodology that helps in analysis and research of naturally occurring language through the help of computerized corpora, i.e. with the specialized software. From the very beginning, modern corpus linguistics has been closely associated with the development of computer software for corpus analysis. In modern corpus linguistics, the linguists and the computer scientists share a common goal that it is important to depend on the real or actual language data (speech or written) for carrying out any kind of linguistic analysis. Moreover, it is an approach which satisfies two main purposes: how people use language in day-to-day communication and to build up intelligent system to interact with human beings.

It is not easy to classify corpora into various types. Modern day corpora are of various types. In fact, it is a very crucial task of classifying language corpora into different types. However, written corpus, spoken corpus, general corpus, monolingual corpus, bilingual corpus, unannotated corpus, annotated corpus, parallel and learner corpus are worth mentioning.

2 Related Studies

The first computer corpus, "Brown Corpus" was created early in the 1960s by Nelson Francis and Henry Kuccera. But it was not warmly accepted by the linguistics community, yet they are regarded as the pioneer of the Corpus linguistics. Creation of corpus is the most important to keep alive from the extinction of languages from this world. Keeping in the notice for the development of the Indian scheduled languages the government of India also started corpus generation revolution in India. As a consequence of its view the government of India emphasized for the development of Indian scheduled languages in technological media world and initiated the technological development works on scheduled languages in 1991. Accordingly machine readable texts have been developed in some major languages in India viz. Hindi, Indian English, Punjabi, Telugu, Kannada, Malayalam, Marathi, Gujarati, Oriya, Bengali, Assamese, Sanskrit, Urdu, Sindhi and Kashmiri in many universities and technology Institutes of India. Later development of corpora for the remaining languages had been done as to run parallel with the other languages for the better gaining to all.

Bodo language belongs to the Sino Tibetan language family under the sub branch of Assam-Burmese group. This language speakers have spread highly in the northern part of the Brahmaputra valley. They are also scattered in all the districts of Assam state more or less. Apart from they can be found in the North-Eastern states like Arunachal, Nagaland, Mizoram, Manipur, Tripura, Northern parts of West Bengal, Bihar and adjoining part of the Bangladesh, Nepal and Bhutan in small concentration. This language has the three distinct dialects according to some researchers. But Promod Chandra Bhattachrya in his doctoral thesis book "A descriptive analysis of the Boro Language" stated four dialects of Bodo language. These are i)

---

1. Crystal, David. 1992. *An Encyclopedic Dictionary of Language and Languages.* Oxford,85 (cf.)

North-west dialects areas having sub dialects of North Kamrupand North Goalpara district ii) South-West dialect area comprising South Goalpara and garo hills district iii) North-Central Assam dialect area comprising Darrang lakhimpur districts and a few places of Arunachal Pradesh iv) Southern dialect area comprising Nowgong North Cachar , Mikir Hills, Cachar and adjacent districts. It has two types of tone high and low tone. Intonation, juncture, agglutinating features is there in this language. Use of high back unrounded /w/ vowel is more frequent in this language. There are 22 phonemes 16 consonant and 6 vowel phonemes. Highly use of monosyllabic word can be found in this language. Devnagiri script is the main script of this language.

Recently the language has recognized as the scheduled language by the government of India in 2003. The language is the medium of instruction up to the 10th standard in school from 1963. In 1984 the language is recognized as the state associate official language in the districts of Kokrajhar and Udalguri. This language is introduced as major subject in the colleges under Gauhati University affiliation in the very recent.

3 Bodo Text Corpus

Consideration of size or length of corpus is an important factor. Overall size of Bodo corpus is determined as 1.5 million words. It is also determined of the availability of data, time for computerizing them in the format. The determined size of the corpus is collected from the expected three main category- Media, Learned and Literature. These categories are again classified into sub categories during the creation of Bodo corpus as given against in the following table. Thus the corpus generation is done keeping in mind of determined target from the different domain collection resources in Bodo. In Bodo media house collection news paper like dailies, weeklies; bi-weeklies and magazines monthlies, bi-monthlies etc are very less. And medical science, engineering, technological word terms very rare, those terms words are taken from the "Glossary of Administrative Terms" published by the Ministry of Human Resource Development (Department of Higher Education), government of India. Entire collection of the data was taken from the written texts document from the various resources as given in the following tree diagram. In Media category total 637000 roots words have been entered comprising category and subcategories. 229250 root words from the learned material category including category and sub categories and a total count of 711500 root words from literature category have been computerised in the text format as shown in the following tree diagram. Having all these three category the Bodo corpus has been created and shaped a total word counting of 1.5 million words (total 1,577,750 words).

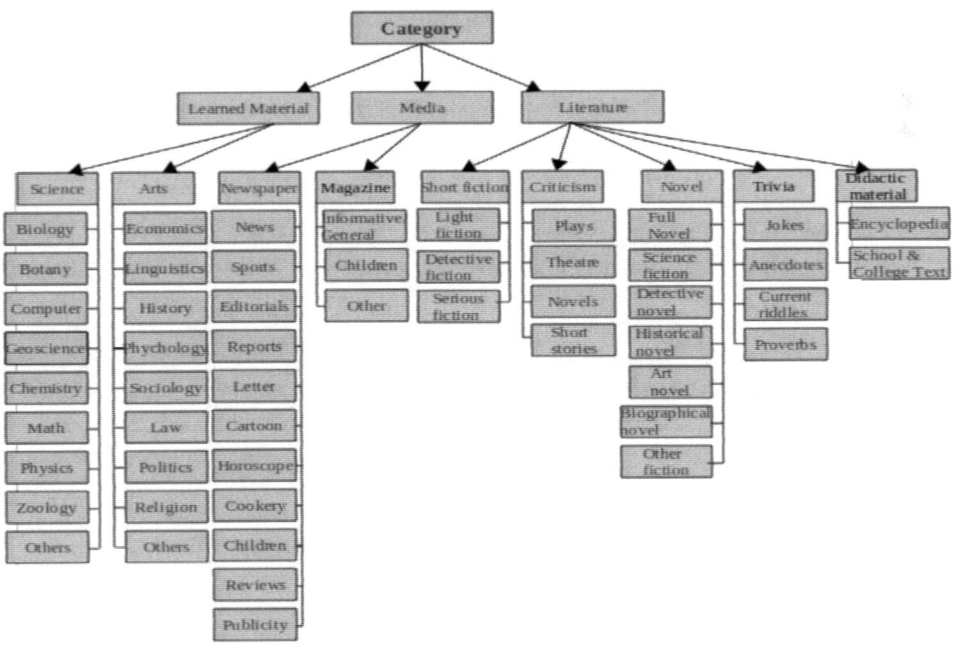

FIGURE 1 – A tree diagram showing categories of corpus contents

3.1 Content Selection

A large number of written genres are selected keeping in the mind of its purpose and utility of a corpus. But poetry genre is not included in our selection. Some genres are not in Bodo like Obituaries, Classified advertisements in the news paper. So these are cannot be found in the format data. There is no film's and women's magazine in Bodo but getting a few representations in the magazines it was included in the corpus. All these genres represent the actual sense of the language and they are listed in the above given diagram.

It is the second task after selecting the genres to determine how many the numbers of texts and the range of writers to be included in the Bodo corpus. There are a huge number of texts available in the languages, but we are very selective in determining the number of texts. Similarly, in the selection of the range of authors, we give importance to both eminent authors and little-known authors. But in case of news paper and magazine we select all the news papers and magazines published in Bodo as news paper items are not available in the language. In case of learned material also we try to cover up all necessary domains. And in literature the science fiction and sentimental fiction are also not available, so they are avoided in the corpus while generating the corpora.

3.2 Data Collection

For building a corpus in Bodo, data are collected from the written texts of the language. In order to collect data, we mainly go for buying books, use of library materials, some texts are also photocopied and scanned etc. The issue of copyright is always kept in mind.

3.3 Computerizing data

The collected data are now ready for entering on to the computer. The task of computerising the text materials is a very crucial. These data are compiled by the native speakers only. Trio-lingual a (Bodo-English-Hindi) dictionary of Bodo Sahitya Sabha published by Onsumwi Library, Kokrajhar, Assam is followed while entering the texts in the format for standardization of the language and in some cases linguistics standardization is also followed.

3.4 Validation

The next process is the validation of those typed data. Validation must be done by the expert. He should be a native speaker of Bodo langauge who has the linguistic command over the Bodo langauge. Generation of Bodo corpus is based the standardization of "Boro-Ingraji-Hindi Swdwbbigung" a trio-lingual (Bodo-English-Hindi) dictionary of Bodo Sahitya Sabha published by Onsumwi Library, Kokrajhar, Assam and in some cases linguistics standardization is also followed. Present discussion is done generated raw corpus in Bodo of few years back. Validation is done manually because this language does not have still tagged corpus and annotated texts. It has a long way to reach its fruitful goal.

4 Issues related to Bodo corpus generation

The size and quality of the corpus depends on the data of a respective language on its resources. Bodo does not have such a rich resources in various fields of its language and the literature and in the science (Chemistry, physics etc.) and in the media house whatever it is electronics or print media. Child literature is very less as compared to other literature and medical science and engineering and the terms of respective subject's words are very rare. Medical science, administrative engineering terms words are entered in the corpus from the glossary book published by MHRD, government of India. Provisions like obituary, classified advertisements etc. are not there in the news paper. In these entire field the resources is increasing day to day. Here we mention some challenges faced during building period of Bodo corpus:

Spelling variation

It is a major problem in Bodo literature as well as in other writing fields also. No standard or uniform spelling system is followed by the authors or writers in this language for their writings though standardized language is followed. Many authors and writers go their own wishes. So it is found very difficult while entering texts documents in the format. As for example: [थाखाय, थाखाइ (*thakhai*): for], [बायदि, बाइदि

(*baidi*): etc.] here whereas both the word [थाखाय, थाखाइ (*thakhai*): for] is used to mean the same meaning but spelling is changed in the last letter of the word i.e. य letter is changing to इ in the second word and also in second example [बायदि, बाइदि (*baidi*): alike] it also refers same meaning though the word spelling in the middle is changed from य to इ. Both in the above example there is no change in their word meaning but its spelling is varying in both the words. So it is one of the major problems which one has to be follow while entering the text for corpus.

Word Split

Splitting of words is found frequently in Bodo while entering the texts into format. These words are edited and correctly entered by the compiler. For example:

BS: बुंदोंमोन दि TF:bungdwngmw di

Correct:BS: बुंदोंमोनदि TF:bungdwngmwdi

Joined Sentence/Word

Many times joined sentence is found in the texts while entering the texts. The compiler itself corrected the sentence and entered in the format.

BS: गस्लाखौ गानहां जाबायमोन।रामोना आंखौ लिंहरो।

TF:goslakhou ganhan jabaimwn.Ramwna angkhou linghorw

Correct:BS: गस्लाखौ गानहां जाबायमोन। रामोना आंखौ लिंहरो।

TF:goslakhou ganhan jabaimwn. Ramwna angkhou linghorw.

Punctuation Error

A large number of punctuation incorrect marks are found in the texts materials. These are removed and corrected by the compiler. As for example

BS: खोलाहा थिङै। सानैजों गोबालायासै । TF: khwlaha thingwi. Sanwijwng gwbalayaswi.

Correct:BS: खोलाहा थिङै सानैजों गोबालायासै। TF: khwlaha thingwi sanwijwng gwbalayaswi.

Dialect Words

Sometime many dialect words are found in the texts. These words are corrected by the compiler and entered in the data format for the corpus. For instance

BS: कोरर्टारखो TF: quarterkhw

Correct:BS: कोरर्टारखौ TF:quarterkhou

Grammatical error

There are lots of sentences which are found grammatically incorrect in the texts. Those sentences are edited and entry is done correctly by the compiler as given in the following example.

BS: जेब्ला रांरासिया गहेल थानाय कोरर्टारखो मोनहैयो अब्ला हर 10 टासो जाबायमोन ।

TF: jebla rangrasiya gohel thanai quarterkhou mwnhwiyw obla hor 10 tasw jabaimwn

Correct:BS: जेब्ला रांरासिया गहेल थानाय कोरर्टारखौ मोनहैयो अब्ला हरनि 10 टासो जाबायमोन ।

TF: jebla rangrasiya gohel thanai quarterkhou mwnhwiyw obla horni 10 tasw jabaimwn.

Hyphenated words

Bodo also have hyphenated words, those are in case of multiword expression words. But surprisingly, there are a few hyphenated words in Bodo within a word which are found in the texts. Those words are compiled and entered by the compiler in the format. For example

BS: गामि-आरिफ्रा TF: gami-arifra

Correct:BS: गामिआरिफ्रा TF: gamiarifra

Incomplete sentence

Incomplete sentences in the texts are very frequent in the Bodo texts. Complier has to face problem . For instance

BS: बियो गाज्लं Ø थाङो । TF: biyw gajlaong Ø thangw.

Correct:BS: बियो गाज्लं गाज्लं थाङो। TF: biyw gajlong gajlong thangw.

Conclusion

It is seen from the above discussion that there is no developed fonts in Bodo. Due to in-uniformity of spelling the compiler of the corpus has to face several problems while entering the text into the format. In such cases they have to correct themselves. There is no science and sentimental fictions in Bodo and in some fields like journals like women's, children's, whether it is monthlies, bi-monthlies and news papers whether it is dailies, weeklies etc are very rare. The entire generation of Bodo corpus is based the standardization of trio-lingual (a Bodo-English-Hindi) dictionary of Bodo Sahitya Sabha published by Onsumwi Library, Kokrajhar, Assam in some cases and linguistics standardization is also followed. Present discussion is done generated raw corpus in Bodo of few years back. Validation of this generation corpus is done manually as this language does not have still tagged corpus and annotated texts. It has a long way to reach its fruitful goal.

References

Brahma, Promod Chandra (Compiler): *Boro-Ingraji-Hindi Swdwbbigung*, Onsumwi Library 2003, Kokrajhar Assam.

Ministry of Human Resource Department. Government of India 2007, *Glossary of Administrative Terms*

Aston, G (Ed. 2004) *Learning with Corpora.* Cambridge: Cambridge University press.

Jayaram, B.D and Rajyashree, S.K.: *Corpora in Indian Languages. Central Institute of Languages Manasagangotri,* Mysore 570006, India.

Jayaram, B.D. (1996). *Development of Corpora in Indian Languages: Problems and Suggested Solutions.* Paper presented at workshop of Indian Language Corpus and its applications at CIIL, Mysore.

Ganesan, M: *Tamil Corpus Generation and Text Analysis:* Annamalai University, Annamalainagar, Tamilnadu, India.

Jaimai Purev and Chimeddorj Obdayar. (2008). *Corpus Building for Mongolian Language* in Proceedings The 6th Workshop on Asian Languae Resources, 2008

Steven A. and Steven B. (2010). *The Human Language Project: building a universal corpus of the world's languages.* In Proceedings of the 48th Annual Meeting of the Association for Computational Linguistics, Uppsala, Sweden.

N.S. Dash (2005). Corpus Languistics and Language Technology with Reference to Indian languages: Mitali Publication, New Delhi.

Charles F. Mayer: English Corpus Linguistics An Introduction. Published by the press Syndicate of the University of Cambridge.

Stella E.O. Tagnin: A Multilingual Learner Corpus in Brazil. Published: Rodopi.

McEnery and Andrew Wilson: Corpus Linguistics. Published by Edinburge University press.

Michael McCarthy: Touchstone From Corpus to Course Book. Published by the syndicate of the University of Cambridge.

Kenji Imamura and Eiichiro Sumita (2002). Bilingual Corpus Cleaning Focusing on Translation Literality. In: 7th International Conference on Spoken Language Processing (ICSLP-2002).

Dependency Parsers for Persian

Mojgan Seraji[1] *Beata Megyesi*[2] *Joakim Nivre*[3]
(1 & 2 & 3) Uppsala University, Department of Linguistics and Philology
`firstname.lastname@lingfil.uu.se`

ABSTRACT
We present two dependency parsers for Persian, MaltParser and MSTParser, trained on the Uppsala PErsian Dependency Treebank. The treebank consists of 1,000 sentences today. Its annotation scheme is based on Stanford Typed Dependencies (STD) extended for Persian with regard to object marking and light verb contructions. The parsers and the treebank are developed simultanously in a bootstrapping scenario. We evaluate the parsers by experimenting with different feature settings. Parser accuracy is also evaluated on automatically generated and gold standard morphological features. Best parser performance is obtained when MaltParser is trained and optimized on 18,000 tokens, achieving 68.68% labeled and 74.81% unlabeled attachment scores, compared to 63.60% and 71.08% for labeled and unlabeled attachment score respectively by optimizing MSTParser.

KEYWORDS: Persian dependency treebank, dependency parsing, Farsi, Persian, MaltParser, MSTParser.

1 Introduction

Data-driven tools for syntactic parsing have been successfully developed and applied to a large number of languages. The existing data-driven syntactic parsers are based on phrase structure, dependency structure, or specific linguistic theories such as HPSG, LFG or CCG. Dependency-based representations have become more widely used in the recent decade, as the approach seems better suited than phrase structure representations for languages with free or flexible word order (Kübler et al., 2009). Dependency parsing, in addition, has been shown to be useful in language technology applications, such as machine translation and information extraction, when detecting the underlying syntactic pattern of a sentence, because of their transparent encoding of predicate-argument structure (Kübler et al., 2009).

This paper presents the adaptation and evaluation of two dependency parsers, MaltParser (Nivre et al., 2006) and MSTParser (McDonald et al., 2005a) for Persian. The parsers are trained on a syntactically annotated corpus developed for Persian; the Uppsala PErsian Dependency Treebank (UPEDT) (Seraji et al., 2012).

The paper is organized as follows. Section 2 briefly describes the structure and the characteristics of the Persian language, followed by a description of the dependency structure and the functional annotation of the Persian dependency treebank on which the data-driven parsers are trained. A short description of MaltParser and MSTParser ends the section. Section 3 introduces the design of our experiments and Section 4 presents the results of the evaluation covering the results of MaltParser and MSTParser, as well as an error analysis for the developed parsers. Finally, Section 5 concludes the paper.

2 Background

2.1 Persian

Persian belongs to the Indo-Iranian languages, a branch of the Indo-European family. The writing system is based on the Arabic alphabet consisting of 28 letters and four additional letters. Persian is written from right to left and Persian morphology is regulated by an affixal system, see more on Persian orthography and morphology in Seraji et al. (2012).

Persian has a SOV word order and is verb final. The head word usually follows its dependents. However, the syntactic relations have a mixed typology, as prepositions always precede their nominal dependent. Sentences consist of an optional subject and object followed by a compulsory verb, i.e., (S) (O) V. Subjects, however, can be placed anywhere in a sentence or they may completely be omitted as Persian is a pro-drop language with an inflectional verb system (where the verb is inflected for person and number). The use and the order of the optional constituents are relatively arbitrary and this scrambling characteristic makes Persian word order highly flexible. Verbs are usually compounds consisting of a preverbal element such as a noun, adjective, preposition, or adverb combined with a bleached or light verb. Light verbs and passive constructions may be split by other intervening elements such as subjunctives, adjectives, future auxiliaries, and negations, that might cause crossing dependencies in syntactic annotation.

2.2 Persian Treebank

Uppsala PErsian Dependency Treebank (UPEDT) (Seraji et al., 2012) is a dependency-based syntactically annotated corpus consisting of 1,000 sentences and 19,232 tokens (14,397 types), which is available in CoNLL-format. The data is taken from the open source, validated corpus UPEC (Seraji et al., 2012) created from on-line material containing newspaper articles and common texts with different genres and topics such as fiction, as well as technical descriptions and texts about culture and art. The corpus is annotated with morpho-syntactic and partly semantic features. The aim is to expand the treebank with 10,000 sentences in the near future by using data-driven dependency parsers for bootstrapping, and manual validation of the annotation.

In the treebank, each head and dependent relation is marked and annotated with functional categories, indicating the grammatical function of the dependent to the head. The treebank annotation scheme is based on Stanford Typed Dependencies (STD) which has become a de facto standard for English today (Marneffe and Manning, 2008). The STD annotation scheme has been applied to Persian and was extended to cover all syntactic relations that are not covered by the original scheme developed for English. Five new labels were added to describe various relations in light verb constructions, and the accusative marker. The added relations are introduced below with a description. The entire annotation scheme can be found in Table 1 where the extended relations introduced for Persian are marked in italic.[1]

***acc*: accusative marker**
An accusative marker is a clitic attached to the direct object of a transitive verb.

***acomp-lvc*: adjectival complement in light verb construction**

[1] An alternative to introducing special relations for the nonverbal elements in light verb constructions would have been to use the *mwe* relation for multi-word expression. However, because light verb constructions are so prevalent in Persian, we chose to distinguish them from other multi-word expressions like compound prepositions and conjunctions.

An adjectival complement in a light verb construction is a preverbal adjective combining with a light verb to form a lexical unit.

***dobj-lvc*: direct object in light verb construction**
A direct object in a light verb construction is a preverbal direct object combining with a light verb to form a lexical unit.[2]

***nsubj-lvc*: nominal subject in light verb construction**
A nominal subject in a light verb construction holds between a preverbal nominal subject combining with a light verb to form a lexical unit (usually with a passive meaning).

***prep-lvc*: prepositional modifier in light verb construction**
A prepositional modifier in a light verb construction is a preverbal prepositional phrase combining with a light verb to form a lexical unit.

In order to increase the size of the treebank, we adapt two freely available dependency parsers that have so far been successfully used for different languages, namely MaltParser (Nivre et al., 2006) and MSTParser (McDonald et al., 2005b), to the Persian dependency treebank.

2.3 Data-Driven Dependency Parsers

MaltParser (Nivre et al., 2006) is an open source data-driven parser generator for dependency parsing. The parser is an implementation of *inductive dependency parsing* (Nivre, 2006) and can be used to develop a parser for a new language given a dependency treebank representing the syntactic relations of that language. The system is characterized as *transition-based*, allowing the user to choose different parsing algorithms and to define optional feature models indicating lexical features, part-of-speech features and dependency type features. The main parsing algorithms available in MaltParser are Nivre's algorithms, including the arc-eager and arc-standard versions described in Nivre (2003) and Nivre (2004), Covington's algorithms, containing the projective and non-projective versions described by Covington (2001), and Stack algorithms, including the projective and non-projective versions of the algorithm described in Nivre (2009) and Nivre et al. (2009). The Covington and the Stack algorithms can handle non-projective trees whereas the Nivre algorithm does not (Ballesteros and Nivre, 2010). For the optimization of MaltParser we used MaltOptimizer (Ballesteros and Nivre, 2010) developed specifically to optimize MaltParser for new data sets with respect to parsing algorithm and feature selection.

MSTParser (McDonald et al., 2005b,a) is also an open source system but based on the graph-based approach to dependency parsing using global learning and exact (or nearly exact) inference algorithms. A graph-based parser extracts the highest scoring spanning tree from a complete graph containing all possible dependency arcs, using a scoring model that decomposes into scores for smaller subgraphs of a tree. MSTParser implements first- and second-order models, where subgraphs are single arcs and pairs of arcs, respectively, and provides different algorithms for projective and non-projective trees.

MaltParser and MSTParser were the top scoring systems in the CoNLL 2006 shared task on multilingual dependency parsing (Buchholz and Marsi, 2006) and has since been applied to a wide range of languages.

[2]Note that this unit may in turn take a direct object. Hence the need to distinguish the light verb object from an ordinary direct object.

Category	Description
acc	*accusative marker*
acomp	adjectival complement
acomp-lvc	*adjectival complement in light verb construction*
advcl	adverbial clause modifier
advmod	adverbial modifier
amod	adjectival modifier
appos	appositional modifier
aux	auxiliary
auxpass	passive auxiliary
cc	coordination
ccomp	clausal complement
complm	complementizer
conj	conjunction
cop	copula
dep	dependent
det	determiner
dobj	direct object
dobj-lvc	*direct object in light verb construction*
mark	marker
mwe	multi-word expression
neg	negation modifier
nn	noun compound modifier
npadvmod	noun phrase as adverbial modifier
nsubj	nominal subject
nsubj-lvc	*nominal subject in light verb construction*
nsubjpass	passive nominal subject
num	numerical structure
number	element of compound number
parataxis	parataxis
pobj	object of a preposition
poss	possession modifier
predet	predeterminer
prep	prepositional modifier
prep-lvc	*prepositional modifier in light verb construction*
punct	punctuation
quantmod	quantifier phrase modifier
rcmod	relative clause modifier
rel	relative
root	root
tmod	temporal modifier
xcomp	open clause complement

Table 1: Syntactic relations in UPEDT based on Stanford Typed Dependencies including extensions for Persian.

3 Parsing Persian

We trained the two parsers by applying various algorithms and feature settings on 1,000 sentences of the Persian dependency treebank. 90% of data was used for training and validation and 10% of the data taken from different topics for final test. To find out what impact a PoS tagger has on the parsing results, we trained the parsers by using gold standard PoS tags taken from UPEC, as well as automatically generated morphological features during training and test. For the automatic morphological annotation, we used TagPer, a freely available part of speech tagger for Persian (Seraji et al., 2012). TagPer was developed by using HunPoS (Halácsy et al., 2007) trained on UPEC consisting of 2,698,274 tokens and has proven to give state-of-the-art accuracy of 97.8% for PoS tagging of Persian (Seraji et al., 2012). TagPer was retrained for our experiments in order to exclude treebank data to avoid data overlap. The results performed by the new TagPer revealed an overall accuracy of 96.1%.[3]

3.1 MaltParser

In order to obtain the highest possible accuracy, given the small data set, we experimented with different algorithms and feature settings to optimize MaltParser. For the optimization, we used the freely available optimization tool for MaltParser, namely MaltOptimizer (Ballesteros and Nivre, 2010). We also used the parser out of the box with its default settings. In addition, we trained the parser with gold standard PoS tags as well as with auto generated PoS tags. In all experiments we used 90% of the treebank data set for training and validation by applying 10-fold cross-validation.

The results are shown in Table 2. Parser optimization leads to improved labeled and unlabeled attachment scores and label accuracy. MaltOptimizer ended up with different algorithms for the different folds during cross validation with best results shifting between *Nivre's algorithms* and *Covington's algorithms*.

We can note that using gold standard PoS features during training and test (DGG and OGG) gives higher attachment scores compared to auto generated PoS tags (DAA and OAA) independently of whether the parser is optimized or not. Higher results are obtained when the parser is trained and tested on automatically genererated PoS features (DAA and OAA), a scenario realistic for parsing new running texts, while accuracy is lowest when the parser is trained on gold-standard features but parses texts that are automatically annotated by a PoS tagger (DGA and OGA).

3.2 MSTParser

To apply MSTParser to Persian, we used the same experiment settings and the same data division, to keep the same criteria as we used for MaltParser. In other words, we continued the validation phase by training MSTParser with its default settings (projective, order 1) and optimized the parser with regards to feature order (order 1 and 2) and non-projective structures. Thus, we combined the training strategies by running the parser in four different experimental settings: projective-order1 (default), projective-order2, non-projective-order1, and non-projective-order2.

The cross-validation results for MSTParser as reported in Table 3 reveal the scores between 62.35% to 65.99% for labeled attachment, and 69.52% to 72.68% for unlabeled attachment.

---

[3]The accuracy of the new TagPer is lower due to the treatment of lvc-construction, multiword expressions, as well as the further correction of UPEC. These corrections were required for our treebank development.

	Default			Optimized		
Including Punct.	**DGG**	**DGA**	**DAA**	**OGG**	**OGA**	**OAA**
Labeled Attachment	68.46	64.80	66.17	**70.39**	66.14	69.37
Unlabeled Attachment	74.07	70.36	71.78	**75.49**	72.19	74.12
Label Accuracy	80.19	78.52	79.81	**83.19**	79.72	81.50

Table 2: Labeled and unlabeled attachment score, and label accuracy score including punctuation of MaltParser in the model selection with different feature settings. DGG = Default with Gold PoS tags in the training and the test set, DGA = Default with Gold PoS tags in the training and Auto PoS tags in the test set, DAA = Default with Auto PoS tags in the training and the test sets, OGG = Optimized with Gold PoS tags in the training and the test set, OGA = Optimized with Gold PoS tags in the training and Auto PoS tags in the test set, and OAA = Optimized with Auto PoS tags in the training and the test set

The optimized versions (OGG, OGA, and OAA), as could be predicted, achieved higher accuracy compared to the default settings (DGG, DGA, and DAA). Highest results on average are achieved by using only projective structures and feature order 2. However, the optimization scores varied slightly between the structures projective-order 2, non-projective-order1 and non-projective-order2 across the folds.

Like MaltParser, the gold standard PoS features (DGG and OGG) give higher attachment scores compared to the auto generated PoS tags (DAA and OAA) independently of whether the MSTParser is optimized or not. Lowest parser performance is obtained when the parser is trained on gold PoS features but tested on automatically generated ones.

	Default			Optimized		
Including Punct.	**DGG**	**DGA**	**DAA**	**OGG**	**OGA**	**OAA**
Labeled Attachment	65.58	62.35	63.78	**65.99**	62.59	64.44
Unlabeled Attachment	72.19	69.52	71.06	**72.68**	69.99	71.80
Label Accuracy	80.37	77.54	78.57	**80.47**	77.43	79.03

Table 3: Labeled and unlabeled attachment score, and label accuracy including punctuation of MSTParser in the model selection with different feature settings (for explanation of the features see Table2).

4 Results

For the final test, we trained the parsers on 90% of the data and tested on a separated, previously unseen test set of 10%. We run the parsers using the feature settings based on their best performance during the validation phase. For MaltParser, we used *nivreeager* algorithm and for the MSTParser, we applied projective training and feature order 2, as these settings had shown the best results on average during the validation phase. The results are given separately with punctuations and without, as shown in Table 4 and Table 5.

Similar to the development experiments, MaltParser obtains highest accuracy in all experiments. The labeled and unlabeled attachment scores reach best result with gold standard PoS tags. However, using automatically generated PoS features during training and test gives higher accuracy compared to when training the parsers on gold-standard PoS but using automatically generated PoS tags on the test data.

Including Punct.	MALT OGG	MALT OGA	MALT OAA	MST OGG	MST OGA	MST OAA
Labeled Attachment	**68.68**	64.05	65.77	63.60	59.94	60.76
Unlabeled Attachment	**74.81**	70.93	73.39	71.08	68.09	68.91
Label Accuracy	**80.64**	76.91	77.50	77.73	74.96	75.78

Table 4: Labeled and unlabeled attachment score, and label accuracy score including punctuation in the model assessment with different feature settings.

Ignoring Punct.	MALT OGG	MALT OGA	MALT OAA	MST OGG	MST OGA	MST OAA
Labeled Attachment	**68.57**	63.54	65.33	63.54	59.20	60.31
Unlabeled Attachment	**75.55**	71.38	73.94	72.06	68.48	69.59
Label Accuracy	**78.28**	73.94	74.70	74.62	71.47	72.40

Table 5: Labeled and unlabeled attachment score, and label accuracy score ignoring punctuation in the model assessment with different feature settings.

In order to provide a more fine-grained analysis of the parsing results for the individual structures, Table 6 displays labeled recall and precision for the 15 most frequently occurring dependency types. As we see, the results vary greatly for both parsers across the relation types. For MaltParser, there is a variation for recall ranging from 46.94% for clausal complement (ccomp) to 91.43% for determiner (det), and for precision from 51.11% for clausal complement to 88.89% for adjectival modifier (amod). For MSTParser, recall is ranging from 34.69% for clausal complement (ccomp) to 92.31% for object for a preposition (pobj), and precision is varying between 36.17% for clausal complement (ccomp) to 88.89% for object for a preposition (pobj).

MaltParser and MSTParser show similar results only for a few relations, which include possessive (poss) and adjectival (amod) modifier, copula (cop), direct object in light verb construction (dobj-lvc), and determiner (det). MaltParser assigns the relation determiner (det) followed by adjectival modifier (amod) to be the candidates of having the highest scores for both recall and precision, while MSTParser assigns object of a preposition (pobj) with the highest F-score. Furthermore, conjunction (conj), direct object (dobj), and the clausal complement (ccomp), are selected as the most erronous relations, although there are differences in the precision and recall figures achieved by the parsers. MaltParser outperforms MSTParser in all cases except for the detection and correctness of objects of a preposition (pobj), and slightly better recall for prepositional modifiers (prep) and coordinating conjunctions (cc).

5 Conclusion

In this paper we have presented two parsers developed for Persian using existing data-driven dependency parsers, MaltParser and MSTParser trained on the Uppsala PErsian Dependency Treebank. The development of the parsers and the treebank has been accomplished simultanously using bootstrapping. As the next step and the highest priority of our future directions involve further annotation and development of our treebank to improve the parsing accuracy.

		MALT		MST	
DepRel	**Freq**	**Rec**	**Prec**	**Rec**	**Prec**
pobj	104	89.42	86.11	92.31	88.89
prep	103	62.14	62.14	63.11	59.09
root	101	80.20	72.32	68.32	69.00
nsubj	99	61.62	55.45	51.52	50.00
poss	97	77.32	65.79	77.32	59.06
advmod	65	63.08	69.49	53.85	60.34
conj	58	50.00	54.72	36.21	44.68
dobj	56	51.79	61.70	41.07	50.00
cc	55	61.82	68.00	63.64	62.50
amod	54	88.89	88.89	83.33	78.95
cop	53	64.15	72.34	64.15	57.63
ccomp	49	46.94	51.11	34.69	36.17
dobj-lvc	43	88.37	69.09	88.37	74.51
det	35	91.43	84.21	91.43	84.21
acc	34	82.35	82.35	73.53	73.53

Table 6: Labeled recall and precision achieved by MaltParser and MSTParser for the 15 most frequent dependency types in the test set.

Acknowledgments

We would like to thank Jon Dehdari for his generosity, sharing his annotation scheme and a set of annotated sentences as a commencement for our treebank annotation effort. We are also grateful to Carina Jahani for her fruitful comments and deliberation regarding Persian grammar. Furthermore, we are particularly grateful to Recorded Future Inc. for their financial support in developing the treebank. The first author has been partly supported by Swedish Graduate School in Language Technology (GSLT).

References

Ballesteros, M. and Nivre, J. (2010). Maltoptimizer: A system for maltparser optimization. In *Proceedings of the 8th international conference on Language Resources and Evaluation (LREC)*, pages 833–841.

Buchholz, S. and Marsi, E. (2006). CoNLL-X shared task on multilingual dependency parsing. In *Proceedings of the Tenth Conference on Computational Natural Language Learning (CoNLL)*, pages 149–164.

Covington, M. A. (2001). A fundamental algorithm for dependency parsing. In *Proceedings of the 39th Annual ACM Southeast Conference*, pages 95–102.

Halácsy, P., Kornai, A., and Oravecz, C. (2007). HunPos: an open source trigram tagger. In *Proceedings of the 45th Annual Meeting of the ACL on Interactive Poster and Demonstration Sessions (ACL)*, pages 209–212.

Kübler, S., McDonald, R., and Nivre, J. (2009). *Dependency Parsing*. Morgan & Claypool Publishers series.

Marneffe, M.-C. D. and Manning, C. D. (2008). Stanford typed dependencies representation. In *Proceedings of the COLING'08 Workshop on Cross-Framework and Cross-Domain Parser Evaluation*, pages 1–8.

McDonald, R., Crammaer, K., and Pereira, F. (2005a). Online large-margin training of dependency parsers. In *Proceedings of the 43rd Annual Meeting of the Association for Computational Linguistics (ACL)*, pages 91–98.

McDonald, R., Pereira, F., Ribarov, K., and Hajic, J. (2005b). Non-projective dependency parsing using spanning tree algorithms. In *Proceedings of the conference on Human Language Technology and Empirical Methods in Natural Language (HLT/EMNLP)*, pages 523–530.

Nivre, J. (2003). An efficient algorithm for projective dependency parsing. In *Proceedings of the 8th International Workshop on Parsing Technologies (IWPT)*, pages 149–160.

Nivre, J. (2004). Incrementality in deterministic dependency parsing. In *Proceedings of the Workshop on Incremental Parsing: Bringing Engineering and Cognition Together (ACL)*, pages 50–57.

Nivre, J. (2006). *Inductive Dependency Parsing*. Springer.

Nivre, J. (2009). Non-projective dependency parsing in expected linear time. In *Proceedings of the Joint Conference of the 47th Annual Meeting of ACL and the 4th International Joint Conference on Natural Language Processing of the AFNLP (ACL-IJCNLP)*, pages 351–359.

Nivre, J., Hall, J., and Nilsson, J. (2006). Maltparser: A data-driven parser-generator for dependency parsing. In *Proceedings of the 5th International Conference on Language Resources and Evaluation (LREC)*, pages 2216–2219.

Nivre, J., Kuhlmann, M., and Hall, J. (2009). An improved oracle for dependency parsing with online reordering. In *Proceedings of the 11th International Conference on Parsing Technologies (IWPT'09)*, pages 73–76.

Seraji, M., Megyesi, B., and Nivre, J. (2012). A basic language resource kit for persian. In *Proceedings of the 8th International Conference on Language Resources and Evaluation (LREC)*, Istanbul, Turkey.

A New DOP Model for Phrase-structure Parsing of Persian Sentences

Zahra Sarabi, Morteza Analouie
(1) Iran University of Science and Technology
(2) Iran University of Science and Technology

Z_sarabi@comp.iust.ac.ir, analoui@iust.ac.ir

ABSTRACT

In this paper we employ a most recent approach to Data Oriented Parsing (DOP), which has named Double-Dop, for Persian sentences. Like other DOP models, Double-Dop parser utilizes syntactic fragments of arbitrary size from a treebank to analyse new sentences, but it extracts a restricted yet representative subset of fragments. It uses only those which are encountered at least twice. The accuracy of Double-DOP is well within the range of state-of-the-art parsers currently used in other NLP-tasks, while offering the additional benefits of a simple generative probability model and an explicit representation of grammatical constructions.
Heretofore there isn't any standard parser for Persian language and this work try to employ Double-Dop Method for parsing Persian sentences.

KEYWORDS: Data Oriented Parsing, Persian Language, Tree Substitution Grammar, Parsing, DOUBLE DOP.

1 Introduction

The Data-Oriented Parsing (DOP) framework, is a famous and wide-coverage parsing method which was first proposed by Scha in 1990(Scha 1990) and formalized by Rens Bod (Bod 1992). Its underlying assumption is that human perception of language based on previous language experiences rather than abstract grammar rules. In the most prominent DOP variants, certain subtrees (called fragments) of variable size, are extracted from the parse trees of the treebank during the training process. These fragments are assigned weights between 0 and 1. Fragments can be recombined to assign parse trees to new sentences. The first implementation of DOP, DOP1 (Bod 1992), and its developed versions(e.g.(Bod 2003)) aimed at extracting all subtrees of all trees in the treebank. The total number of constructions, however, is prohibitively large for non-trivial treebanks: it grows exponentially with the length of the sentences, yielding the astronomically large number of approximately 10^{48} for section 2-21 of the Penn WSJ corpus. Later DOP models have used the Goodman transformation(Goodman 1996; Goodman 2003)to obtain a compact representation of all fragments in the treebank (Bod 2003; Bansal and Klein 2010). The transformation was defined for some versions of DOP to an equivalent PCFG-based model, with the number of rules extracted from each parse tree being linear in the size of the trees. Bod has argued for the Goodman transform as the solution to the computational challenges of DOP (e.g.,(Bod 2003)); it is important to realize, however, that the resulting grammars are still very large: WSJ sections 2-21 yield about7.8×10^6 rules in the basic version of Goodman's transform. Moreover, the transformed grammars differ from untransformed DOP grammars in that larger fragments are no longer explicitly represented. This way, an attractive feature of DOP, viz. the explicit representation of the 'productive units' of language, is lost.
In this paper we use a novel DOP model(Double-DOP) in which we extract a restricted yet representative subset of fragments: those recurring at least twice in the treebank(Sangati and Zuidema 2011). The accuracy of Double-DOP is well within the range of state-of-the-art parsers currently used in other NLP-tasks, while offering the additional benefits of a simple generative probability model and an explicit representation of grammatical constructions. This model reduces the number of extracted fragments from the astronomical 10^{48} to around 10^6.
The rest of the paper is structured as follows. In section 2 we describe Formal Specification of DOP model in general and Double-DOP model in detail, which we will use for parsing. In section 3 we illustrate the Implementation phase and the difficulties of Persian sentences parsing which we are encountered and finally we come to conclusion.

2. Data Oriented Parsing

2.1 Formal Specification of DOP

A DOP grammar can be described as a collection T of fragments. Figure 1 shows an example of four fragments that are extracted from the training parse tree depicted in figure 2, belonging to the PTB[1] training corpus. Fragments are defined in such a way that

---

[1] Persian Treebank (Per TreeBank) :http://hpsg.fu-berlin.de/~ghayoomi/PTB.html
See also(Ghayoomi 2012)

every node is either a non-terminal leaf (with no more children), or has the exact same children as in the original tree. Since Persian is a right-to-left language, the trees in Figures 1and 2 should be read right-to-left.

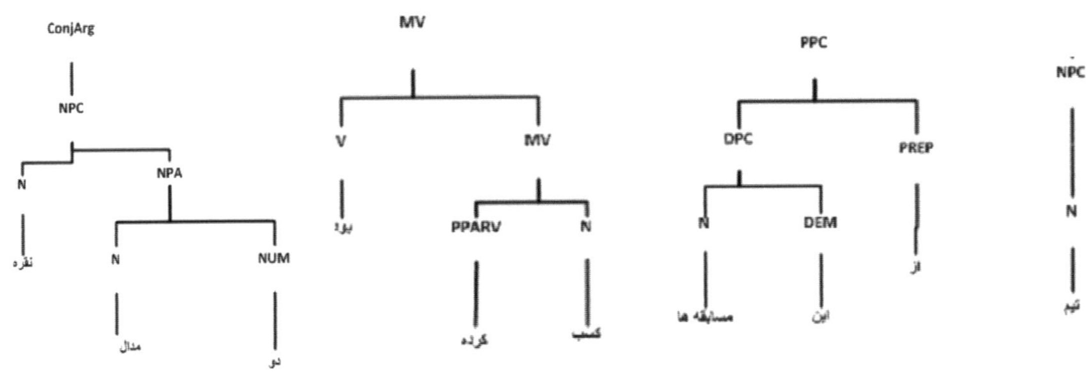

FIGURE 1- Example of elementary trees of depth 4, 3, 3, and 2.

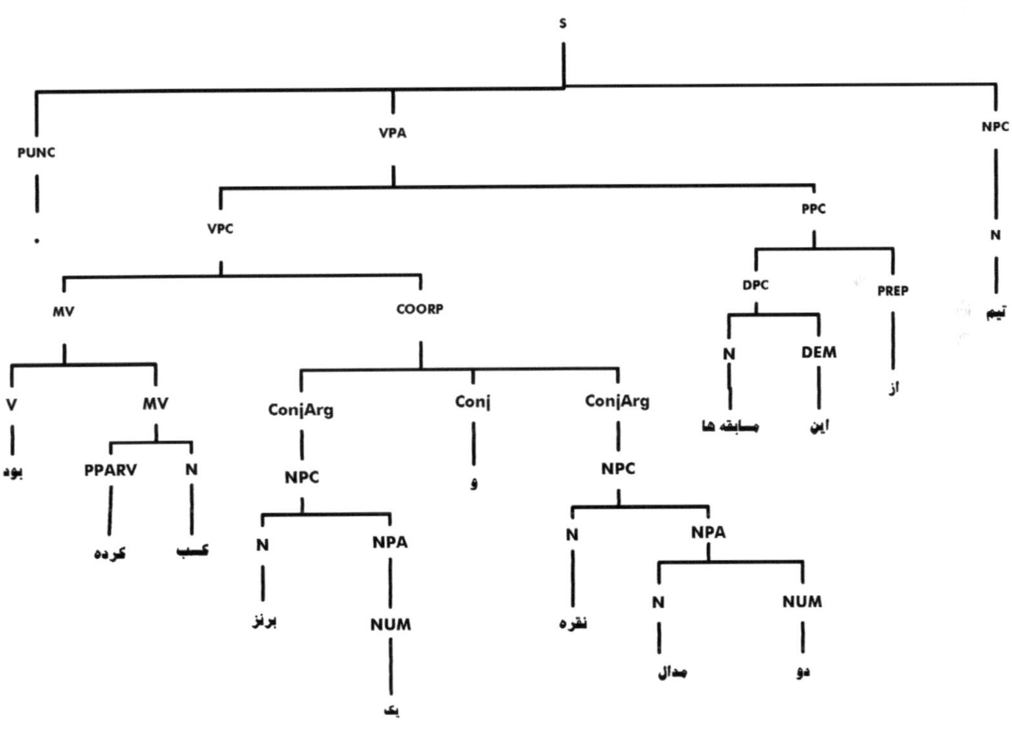

FIGURE 2- Parse tree of the sentence "تیم از این مسابقه‌ها دو مدال نقره و یک برنز کسب کرده بود".

DOP parses new input by combining treebank subtrees by means of a leftmost node-substitution operation, indicated as °. Two subtrees t and u can be combined by means

of the substitution operation, $t \circ u$, if the label on the leftmost nonterminal leaf node of t is identical to the label on the root node of u. The result of this operation is a unified fragment which corresponds to subtree t with the leftmost nonterminal leaf replaced with the entire fragment u. The substitution operation can be applied iteratively since $\circ$ is left associative: $t \circ u \circ z = (t \circ u) \circ z$ (Bod 1998).
The probability of a parse tree is computed from the occurrence frequencies of the subtrees in the treebank. That is, the probability of a subtree t is taken as the number of occurrences of t in the training set, | t |, divided by the total number of occurrences of all subtrees t' with the same root label as t. Let r(t) return the root label of t:

$$P(t) = \frac{|t|}{\sum_{t':r(t')=r(t)} |t'|} \qquad (1)$$

The probability of a derivation $t_1 \circ \ldots \circ t_n$ is computed by the product of the probabilities of its subtrees t_i:

$$P(t1 \circ \ldots \circ tn) = \prod_i P(t_i) \qquad (2)$$

A same parse tree can be generated by a large number of different derivations, which involve different fragments from the corpus. The probability of a parse tree is the probability that it is produced by any of its derivations. These derivations have their own probability of being generated. Therefore, the probability of a parse tree T is the sum of the probabilities of its distinct derivations D:

$$\mathrm{P(T)} = \sum_{\text{D derives T}} \mathrm{P(D)} \qquad (3)$$

A disadvantage of this model is that an extremely large number of subtrees (and derivations) must be taken into account. This leads to exponentially many trees, and thus both exponential time and space requirements. On top of this, the typical optimization criterion, most probable parse, is NP-complete to solve for, leading to an exponentially hard problem of exponential size(Sima'an 1999).The solution has typically been various approximations, such as sampling from the set of all trees, to reduce the size of the grammar, or sampling from the set of all parses – Monte Carlo approximations – to reduce the difficulty of the search. One alternate solution is PCFG-reduction of DOP that generates the same trees with the same probabilities (Goodman 2003).Goodman was able to define a way to convert the DOP grammar in a novel CFG, of which the size increases linearly in the size of the training data. Bod shows that these PCFG-reductions result in a 60 times speedup in processing time w.r.t. DOP1(Bod 2003). However In this case the grammatical constructions are no longer explicitly represented and substantial engineering effort is needed to optimally tune the models and make them efficient.

2.2 Formal Specification of Double-DOP model

The most recent solution to computational challenges of DOP is Double-Dop model which propose a more principled-based approach for explicitly extracting a relatively small but still representative set of fragments from a treebank, i.e., those which are encountered at least twice in the treebank, for which there is evidence about their reusability(Sangati and Zuidema 2011). More precisely the model extracts only the largest shared fragments for all pairs of trees in the treebank. The most important technical contributions of Double-Dop method is: (i) a way to restrict the set of fragments to only those that occur multiple times in the train set, (ii)a transform-backtransform approach that allows using off-the-shelf PCFG parsing techniques.

The first step to build a DOP model is to define the set of elementary fragments in the model. Although extracting recurring fragments is not trivial, but Sangati in(Sangati, Zuidema et al. 2010)proposed a dynamic programming algorithm. The algorithm iterates over every pair of trees in the treebank and looks for common maximal fragments. All subtrees of these extracted fragments necessarily also occur at least twice, but they are only explicitly represented in our extracted set if they happen to form a largest shared fragment from another pair of trees. Figure 3 shows an example of a pair of trees <α,β>, being compared. All the non-terminal nodes of the two trees are indexed following a depth-first ordering. The algorithm builds a chart M with one column for every indexed non-terminal node α_i in α, and one row for every indexed non-terminal node β_j in β. Each cell M<i , j>, identifies a set of indices corresponding to the largest fragment in common between the two trees starting from α_i andβ_j . This set is empty if α_i and β_j differ in their labels, or they do not have the same list of child nodes. Otherwise (if both the labels and the lists of children match) the set is computed recursively as follows:

$$M < i,j > = \{\alpha_i\} \cup \left(\cup_{c=\{1,2,\ldots,|ch(\alpha)|\}} M < ch(\alpha_i, c), ch(\beta_j, c) >\right) \qquad (4)$$

Where ch(α) returns the indices of α's children, and ch(α, c) the index of its cth child.

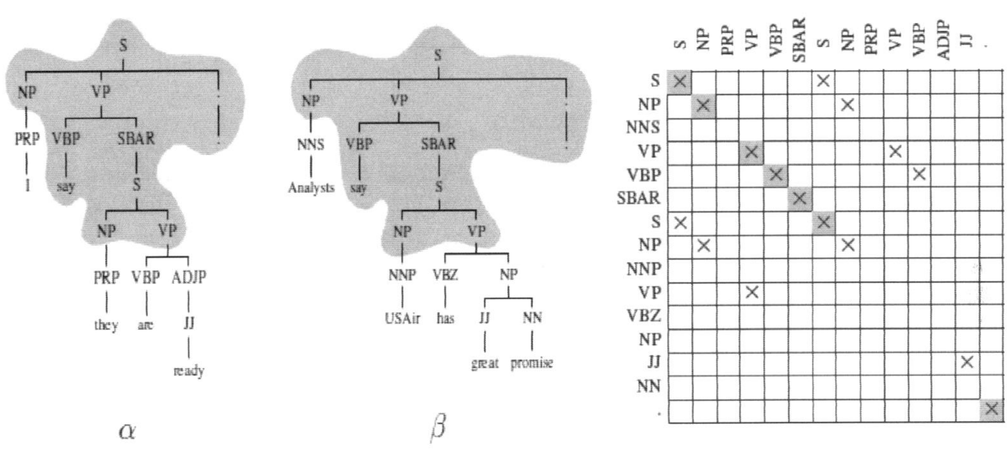

FIGURE 3: Left: example of two trees sharing a single maximum fragment, highlighted in the two trees. Right: the chart used in the algorithm to extract all maximum fragments shared between the two trees(Sangati and Zuidema 2011)

The number of recurring fragments in this grammar, extracted from the training sections of the Penn WSJ treebank, is around 1 million, and thus is significantly lower than previous work extracting explicit fragments (e.g.,(Bod 2001) used more than 5 million fragments up to depth 14).

2.2.1 Parsing with Double-DOP

It is possible to define a simple transform of probabilistic fragment grammar, such that off-the shelf parsers can be used. In order to perform the PTSG/PCFG conversion, every fragment in the grammar must be mapped to a CFG rule which will keep the same probability as the original fragment. The corresponding rule will have as the left hand side the root of the fragment and as the right hand side its yield, i.e., a sequence of terminals and nonterminals (substitution sites)(Sangati and Zuidema 2011).

2.2.2 Inducing probability distributions

Relative Frequency Estimate (RFE): The simplest way to assign probabilities to fragments is to make them proportional to their counts in the training set.

$$P_{RFE}(f) = \frac{count(f)}{\sum_{f' \in F_{root(f)}} count(f')} \qquad (5)$$

3 Implementation

In this section we want to illustrate the implementation phase in which we employ Double-DOP model to Persian language. For this purpose we have some challenges and difficulties in processing Persian language. In continue we first analyse these challenges and after that explain the detail of our implementation.

3.1 challenges of Persian language processing

Persian language is the formal language of Iran and some neighbourhood countries like Afghanistan and Tajikistan and more than one hundred millions of people speak with this language. Furthermore many written resources like online pages, news, books and translated books exist for this language. So preparing tools and processing resources, which is used in linguistics applications, should take into consideration.

Nowadays the importance of availability or development of annotated data becomes crucial to feed linguistic investigation and also to use data driven approaches in human language technologies. Some languages like English and German are given a great amount of consideration which results to various types of data sources; while some other languages like Persian are less developed in terms of availability of annotated data.
A necessary condition for testing a DOP model is the availability of annotated language corpora. Therefore one of the most important challenges in parsing Persian sentences with data oriented approaches is the lack of linguistic annotated resources like a standard treebank. Until very recently, there wasn't any standard public available treebank for Persian language, but fortunately some efforts being performed by Ghayoomi in Freie Universität Berlin, Germany, who is developing the Persian treebank and make it publicly available as the only readily available corpora consisted of syntactically labeled phrase-structure trees[1](Ghayoomi 2012). This Persian treebank

[1]The developed Persian treebank is accessible from this link: http://hpsg.fu-berlin.de/_ghayoomi/PTB.html

(PTB) currently contains 1012sentences with the total size of 27731 word tokens.Of course in order to employ DOP model, we would need a larger treebank and it seems that the results of our work would become poor relative to the same methodology applied to English treebanks, But that does not detract from the value and efficiency of this approach.

3.2 Experimental setup

In order to build and test our Double-DOP model we employ the Persian treebank-PTB(Ghayoomi 2012).

Preparing the treebank: We start with some pre-processing of the treebank, following standard parsing methods. We named this step preparing the treebank and performed following tasks in this step in order: first we divide the treebank into two sections of train and test and assign about 1000 sentences for train and 200 sentences for test. Next we have removed all empty nodes, functional tags, semantic tags, traces and also punctuations from the treebank. After that we apply binarization procedure to training pars trees of treebank. Binarization is particularly important for generative models like DOP and PCFGs, and was essential for the success of the model, where all the children of an internal node are produced at once. Binarization, in fact, provides a way to generalize flat rules, by splitting it in multiple generation steps. Double-DOP model creators claim that, on an unbinarized treebank, the model performed rather poorly because of the abundance of flat rules. However, our current model uses a strict left binarization as in(Matsuzaki, Miyao et al. 2005).

Executing Fragment seeker algorithm (Sangati, Zuidema et al. 2010):

In this step we explicitly extract a subset of fragments from the training treebank. As explained in section 2, we extract only those fragments that occur two or more times in the treebank. Details of this algorithm illustrated in (Sangati, 2010) and they implemented software for extracting recurring fragments named Fragment Seeker[1]. Although this software was available and free but it didn't work well for Persian language and therefore we implemented the algorithm again for Persian language. Running this algorithm is the most time-consuming step (around 160 CPU hours).Parse trees in the training corpus are not necessarily covered entirely by recurring fragments; to ensure better coverage, we also extract all PCFG-productions not included in the set of recurring fragments.

Parsing

We convert our PTSG into a PCFG (section 2.2.1) and use Bitpar[2] parser (Schmid 2004)to parse the 200 sentences in the test set. Bitpar is a parser that implements the CYK algorithm. It can parse sentences starting from a set of CFG rules. So it's not specific to a certain language.

---

[1]The implemented software for extracting recurring fragments (Fragment Seeker) is available at http://staff.science.uva.nl/~fsangati/

[2] http://www.ims.uni-stuttgart.de/tcl/SOFTWARE/BitPar.html

Results

In this work in order to clarify to what extent Double DOP parsing improves parsing results, we first train a PCFG parser for Persian Treebank as a baseline and achieve only 36% in F-score. We have also compared our best Double-DOP base model with some previous DOP models like DOP-Goodman and DOP $_{h=2}$.

Table 1 shows a summary of the parsing results of our system on Double-DOP model , which achieves 59% in labeled F-score. Further investigations suggest that the majority of parsing errors are due to crossing brackets and wrongly labeled constituents are in fact a minor source of error.

Parsing Model	Result
PCFG(H=1 , P=1)	33%
Stanford PCFG Parser (H=1 P=1)	39%
DOP1	48%
DOP Goodman	50%
DOP $_{h=2}$	49%
Double-DOP	59%

Table 1- Summary of the Parsing evaluation results

Conclusion

We have presented a simplified DOP formalism, named Double-DOP for learning the constituency structure of Persian sentences. Double-DOP is a most recent DOP approach for parsing, which uses all constructions recurring at least twice in a treebank. Other DOP models have many shortcomings so that DOP parsers are almost never used in other NLP tasks. The most important reasons for this are probably the computational inefficiency of many instances of the approach, the lack of downloadable software and the difficulties with replicating some of the key results. Fortunately Double-DOP model untie these difficulties by: the efficient algorithm for identifying the recurrent fragments in a treebank runs in polynomial time. The transformation to PCFGs that the model defines allows us to use a standard PCFG parser, while retaining the benefit of explicitly representing larger fragments.

The results of our work are poor relative to the same methodology applied to English treebanks. One of the main reasons is certainly the smaller size of the training corpus used in the current shared task. As in other types of exemplar-based learning techniques, DOP models require a large amount of data in order to achieve high accuracy.

We try to improve our results in further investigations.

References

Bansal, M. and D. Klein (2010). "Simple, accurate parsing with an all-fragments grammar." Proceedings of the 48th Annual Meeting of the ACL: pages 1098–1107.

Bod, R. (1992). "A computational model of language performance: Data oriented parsing." Proceedings COLING'92 (Nantes, France): pp: 855–859.

Bod, R. (1998). "Beyond Grammar: An Experience-Based Theory of Language." Stanford, CSLI Publications.

Bod, R. (2001). "What is the Minimal Set of Subtrees that Achieves Maximal Parse Accuracy?" Proceedings ACL'2001, Toulouse, France.

Bod, R. (2003). "An efficient implementation of a new DOP model." Proceedings of the tenth conference on European chapter of the Association for Computational Linguistics , Volume 1(EACL'03): PP:19–26.

Ghayoomi, M. (2012). "Bootstrapping the Development of an HPSG-based Treebank for Persian." Linguistic Issues in Language Technology: LiLT.

Goodman, J. (1996). "Efficient algorithms for parsing the DOP model." In Proceedings of the Conference on Empirical Methods in Natural Language Processing,: pages 143–152.

Goodman, J. (2003). "Efficient parsing of DOP with PCFG-reductions." In Bod et al. (2003).

Matsuzaki, T., Y. Miyao, et al. (2005). "Probabilistic CFG with latent annotations." Proceedings of the 43rd Annual Meeting on Association for Computational Linguistics, pages 75–82, Morristown, NJ, USA.

Sangati, F. and W. Zuidema (2011). "A Recurring Fragment Model for Accurate Parsing: Double-DOP." In Proceedings of the 2011 Conference on Empirical Methods in Natural Language Processing,: pages 84–95.

Sangati, F., W. Zuidema, et al. (2010). "Efficiently Extract Recurring Tree Fragments from Large Treebanks." Proceedings of the Seventh conference on International Language Resources and Evaluation (LREC'10),.

Scha, R. (1990). " Taaltheorie en taaltechnologie; competence en performance." Q. A. M. de Kort and G. L. J. Leerdam, editors, Computertoepassingen in de Neerlandistiek, LVVNjaarboek: 7-22.

Schmid, H. (2004). "Efficient parsing of highly ambiguous context-free grammars with bit vectors." Proceedings of COLING 2004, pp. 162{168. Geneva, Switzerland.

Sima'an, K. (1999). "Learning Efficient Disambiguation." PhD thesis, University of Amsterdam, The Netherlands.

A Hybrid Dependency Parser for Bangla

Arnab Dhar, Sanjay Chatterji, Sudeshna Sarkar, Anupam Basu
Department of Computer Sc. & Engineering, Indian Institute of Technology, Kharagpur, India
Email: {arnabdhar,schatt,sudeshna,anupam}@cse.iitkgp.ernet.in

ABSTRACT

In this paper we describe a two-stage dependency parser for Bangla. In the first stage, we build a model using a Bangla dependency Treebank and subsequently this model is used to build a data driven Bangla parser. In the second stage, constraint based parsing has been used to modify the output of the data driven parser. This second stage module implements the Bangla specific constraints with the help of demand frames of Bangla verbs. The features of the words used in both these stages include morphological features like gender, number, person, etc., parts-of-speech tags, chunk tags and named entity tags. The evaluation results show that this two stage parser performs better than one stage parsers.

1 Introduction

Parsing is a method of analyzing the grammatical structures (phrase structure or dependency structure) of a sentence. In this paper we refer parsing to indicate dependency parsing. Parsing has many applications in natural language processing such as, machine translation, anaphora resolution, question answering, etc. Data driven and grammar driven approaches have been used for parsing.

In a data driven parser of a language, a corpus is manually annotated with dependency relations of that language and used to train a model. This manually annotated corpus is referred to as dependency Treebank. In this paper we refer relation and Treebank to indicate dependency relation and dependency Treebank, respectively. In the Bangla Treebank released in Tool Contest of ICON 2009 and 2010 the dependency relations are assigned between chunks where in a chunk, words are related with intra-chunk relations. The data driven parser identifies the inter-chunk relations in the sentence using the model.

Grammar driven parser uses some language specific rules to identify the relations between chunks. These rules can be considered as constraints for dependents of a head words. If an input dependent of a head word satisfies the constraint then the corresponding relation is assigned between the dependent and the head word.

The availability of Treebank and rules on Bangla dependency grammar are limited. Therefore both the data driven and grammar driven dependency parsers often make mistakes in identifying the dependency relations. In this paper, we describe our experiment on correcting the output of a baseline data driven Bangla parser using Bangla specific constraints.

2 Related work

Bharati et al. (1993) has described a constraint based Hindi parser by applying the Paninian framework. They have shown that the Paninian framework gives an account of the relation between the vibhakti and karaka roles in Hindi sentences. Bharati et al. (2002) has also used the computational Paninian framework for parsing Hindi sentences. The Hindi parser is developed based on translating Hindi grammatical constraints to integer programming constraints. This framework may be adapted for other free word order languages like Bangla. The transformations used by them operate on the grammar rules and not on the parse structures. Two stage constraint based approach described in Bharati et al. (2009) shows how intra-clausal and inter-clausal dependency relations are identified for each token in the sentence at two different stages.

Some study on demand frame or verb frame has been attempted on Hindi by Begum et al. (2008). De et al. (2009a) developed 500 Bangla demand frames including mixed verbs, main verbs and their causative forms.

The release of three Indian language Treebanks for Hindi, Bengali and Telugu in the Tool Contests of ICON 2009 and ICON 2010 have encouraged several researchers to work on Indian language parsing. The results of the nine participants of 2009 Tool Contest and six participants of 2010 Tool Contest are summarized in Husain (2009b) and Husain et al. (2010), respectively.

The participants of ICON 2009 Tool Contest have used both the data driven, grammar driven and hybrid approaches. For example, Nivre (2009) have suggested an optimal feature set for Hindi, Bengali and Telugu to be used in MaltParser.A grammar driven approach (constraint based) for Bengali language parsing has been suggested by De et al. (2009b). The approach consists of three steps, first simplify complex and compound sentential structures into simple sentences, then parse the simple structures by satisfying the Karaka demands of the Demand Groups (Verb Groups), and finally rejoin such parsed structures with appropriate links and Karaka labels. They have used 500 demand frames to achieve the highest performance in Bangla parsing. A hybrid approach has been suggested by Chatterji et al. (2009) where data driven parser used as a baseline system and postprocessed using four hard constraints namely (a) TAM based root identification (b) Genitive Marker Based Possessive Relation Identification (c) Resolving "pof" miss identification and (d) Post-position and suffix marker based rules.

The participants of ICON 2010 Tool Contest have also experimented with data driven, grammar driven and hybrid approaches. Kolachina et al. (2010) used data driven parser (MaltParser) where a linear-time algorithm for projective structures has been used as a parsing algorithm. They have also used LIBSVM learner as a learning algorithm and employed the propagation of some features in order to incorporate such features during the parsing process. They have achieved highest overall performance for Bangla in ICON 2010 Tool Contest. A hybrid approach has been proposed by Ghosh et al. (2010) where data driven parser (MaltParser) has been used as a baseline system and based on the errors of the data driven parser they have implemented a set of parsing rules based on vibhakti information.

3 Two stage parsing system

3.1 Motivation

Data driven parser learns the model from the Treebank of the language. Based on this model the parser identifies the dependency relations in the test sentences. If the size of Treebank of a language is limited, then the data driven parser of that language ought to make mistakes.

In Bangla sentences, the positions of the dependents of a head word are relatively less rigid. Both the dependents and the head words (including the root of the sentence) are often dropped in the Bangla sentences. Therefore, sometimes it is not possible for a data driven Bangla parser to correctly identify the relation.

On the other hand, a constraint based parser identifies relations based on a set of rules consisting of features of dependents and head words. For example, De et al. (2009) have proposed a set of Bangla rules by preparing case frames of Bangla verbs. Rule-set can be incrementally enhanced based on the relations required in a particular application such as machine translation.

So, we propose a hybrid parser where the data driven parser gives the baseline parsing in the first stage and the constraint based parser of the second stage may modify the mistakes of the first stage. Hopefully, this parser will give us better performance than the data driven and rule based parsers.

3.2 Overview

In this paper, we propose a two stage parsing system for Bangla. In the first stage, a data driven parser identifies the dependency relations between chunks in a sentence using the model created from the Bangla Treebank released in ICON 2009. We analyze the relations wrongly identified by the data driven parser and identify rules to correct them.

Researchers have tried several techniques and rules for correcting the mistakes of data driven parsers as discussed in Section 2. Researchers have also used case frames for identifying the dependency relations. Case frames show high performance in identifying the dependency relations in Bangla sentences. In this paper we experiment on the effects of case frames in the correction of mistakes of data driven parser.

3.3 Data driven module

The chunks in the Treebank used in the data driven parser has following attributes.

1. HEADWORD: Head word of chunk
2. HEADROOT: Root of head word of chunk
3. MORPH: Morphological features of head word: gender, number, person, animacy, case and vibhakti
4. POS: Part-of-speech tag of head word
5. CHUNK: Chunk tag
6. DEPREL: Dependency relation of that chunk with another chunk

We use the Covington's algorithm as implemented in MaltParser by Nivre (2006, 2007, 2009) for statistically annotating the dependency relations in Bangla sentences. In this algorithm, partially processed part is used for annotating the unprocessed part of a sentence. A stack is used for holding partially processed chunks (tokens) and a buffer is used for holding unprocessed tokens. The unprocessed tokens are annotated based on the features of the processed and unprocessed tokens. We have selected following set of features based on some experiments.

1. A set of POS features over stack and buffer of length 4.
2. A set of WORD features over stack and buffer of length 2.
3. A set of ROOT features over stack and buffer of length 2.
4. A set of CHUNK features over stack and buffer of length 1.
5. A set of POS features over dependents and head of length 1.
6. A set of combinations of the POS and WORD features of length 1.
7. A set of DEPREL features over dependents of length 1.
8. A set of WORD features over dependents and head of length 1.
9. A set of CHUNK features over dependents and head of length 1.
10. A set of MORPH features over stack and buffer of length 2.

The data driven Bangla parser built using these features achieves accuracy of 75.65% (Label Attachment Score).

3.4 Analyzing the mistakes of data driven module

The data driven parser makes mistakes in identifying some relations and attachments. One example sentence with mistakes of the data driven parser is discussed below. The Roman transliteration in Itrans and English translation are also included.

> আমাকে দিল্লি যেতে হবে।
> (AmAke dilli yete habe.)
> [Me Delhi go have-to]
> I have to go to Delhi.

In this example, আমাকে (AmAke)[me] is the Subject (karta) and দিল্লি (dilli) [Delhi] is the Spatial Locative (sthanadhikaran) of the verb যেতে হবে (yete habe) [have to go]. The data driven parser wrongly identifies আমাকে (AmAke) [me] as Object (karma) and দিল্লি (dilli) [Delhi] as Subject (karta). But, this non-transitive verb does not have Object (karma). Rather an animate noun may be used as Subject (karta). Similarly, this verb can't have 0-ending Subject (karta). Rather this noun may be used as Spatial Locative (sthanadhikaran).

This analysis shows that the mistakes made by the data driven parser in identifying the relations can be rectified using the grammar driven rules. We concentrate on correcting the mistakes of the data driven parser in identifying the following relations.

- karta [subject] (k1) and its subcategories
- karma [object] (k2) and its subcategories
- adhikarana [locative] (k7) and its subcategories
- part-of (pof)
- Verb Modifier (vmod)

3.5 Grammar Driven Module

A Grammar driven module is used as a postprocessor in the proposed hybrid system. This module corrects the mistakes made by the Bangla data driven parser by implementing some Bangla specific constraints. We represent these constraints in tabular way. These tabular representations are referred to as demand frames. The table for a verb contains possible relations with its dependents, the necessity of the relations and the features of the corresponding dependents. The necessity of a relation can be mandatory or desirable. The features we store in the demand frames are the vibhaktis, the part-of-speech tags, the named entity tags and the animacy.

For each Tense, Aspect, Modality (TAM) and certain other features of the Bangla verbs we build a set of transformation rules. All the verbs which have same feature follow same set of transformation rules. The transformation rules (with respect to a particular verb feature) identify the required changes in the basic demand frames of verb roots.

Basic demand frame for the Bangla verb root যাওয়া (yAoYA) [go] and transformation rule for the TAM তে_হবে (te_habe) [have-to] are represented in Table 1 and 2, respectively.

Dependency relation	Necessity	Vibhakti	Lexical type	NET	Semantic class
Subject (karta)	M	0	NN|NNP|PRP	0|PERSON	Animate|Inanimate
Spatial Locative (sthanadhikaran)	D	0|এ(e)|য়(Ya)|তে(te)	NN|NNP|PRP	0|LOCATION	0
Temporal Locative (kaladhikaran)	D	0|এ(e)|য়(Ya)|পর(para)	PRP|NN	0|TIMEX	0

TABLE 1 – Basic demand frame for verb যাওয়া (yAoYA) [go]
M: Mandatory, D: Desirable, NN:Noun, NNP:Proper noun, PRP:Pronoun

In Table 1 features of three dependents namely Subject (karta), Spatial Locative (sthanadhikaran), and Temporal Locative (kaladhikaran) for the verb root যাওয়া (yAoYA) [go] are shown. Subject (karta) is mandatory (M) and the other two dependents are desirable (D) for this verb. The possible values of the features are separated by | (pipe) symbol. Zero (0) indicates that the corresponding value of the feature is either Null or unknown.

Dependency relation	Necessity	Vibhakti	Lexical type	NET	Semantic class
Subject (karta)	M	কে(ke)	NN|NNP|PRP	0|PERSON	Animate|Inanimate

TABLE 2 – Transformation rule for the TAM তে_হবে (te_habe) [have-to].
M: Mandatory, NN: Noun, NNP: Proper noun, PRP: Pronoun

The features of Subject (karta) may change if the verb has TAM তে_হবে (te_habe) [have-to]. According to Table 2, the karta of this verb must have কে (ke) vibhakti.

Transformed demand frame for the verb token যেতে হবে (yete habe) [have to go] as shown in Table 3 is prepared from the basic demand frame of Table 1 and the transformation rule of Table 2. The vibhakti of Subject in the basic demand frame is transformed from 0 (Zero) to কে (ke) in the transformed demand frame.

The transformed demand frame is used to check the dependency relations of the verb token with its dependents as given by the data driven module. If a relation does not match with the corresponding entries in the transformed demand frame then we discard that relation. In this case, we find a relation for the dependent token of the discarded relation as follows.

Dependency relation	Necessity	Vibhakti	Lexical type	NET	Semantic class
Subject (karta)	M	কে(ke)	NN|NNP|PRP	0|PERSON	Animate|Inanimate
Spatial Locative (sthanadhikaran)	D	0|এ(e)|য়(Ya)|তে (te)	NN|NNP|PRP	0|LOCATION	0
Temporal Locative (kaladhikaran)	D	0|এ(e)|য়(Ya)|পর(para)	PRP|NN	0|TIMEX	0

TABLE 3 – Transformed demand frame for verb যেতে হবে (yete habe) [have to go]
M: Mandatory, D: Desirable, NN: Noun, NNP: Proper noun, PRP: Pronoun

The transformed demand frames for each verb (except the verb of the discarded relation) of the sentence are loaded. The features of the token are compared to these transformed demand frame entries. The nearest verb of the token whose transformed demand frame entries match with the features of the token is considered. The corresponding relation replaces the discarded relation.

3.6 Analyzing the effects of grammar driven module

The errors generated by the data driven parser for the example mentioned in Section 3.4 is corrected using the rules imposed by the following constraints.

- Based on the suffix (vibhakti) and semantic class value (animate or inanimate) of Subject (karta) of the verb token যেতে হবে (yete habe) [have to go] the relation of the word আমাকে (AmAke) [me] is changed from Object (karma) to Subject (karta).
- Based on the NET value of Spatial Lcative (sthanadhikaran) of the verb token যেতে হবে (yete habe) [have to go] the relation of দিল্লি (dilli) [Delhi] is changed from Subject (karta) to Spatial Locative (sthanadhikaran).

We show some more wrong outputs of the data driven parser and the effect of constraints on these outputs using dependency trees. The corrections in attachments and labels are shown using dotted lines and boldface, respectively.

1. বইটা তাকে দিয়ে বলল কাল পড়িস.
(ba;iTA tAke diYe balala kAla pa.Disa.)
[book him giving said tomorrow read.]
Giving him the book speaker says read tomorrow.

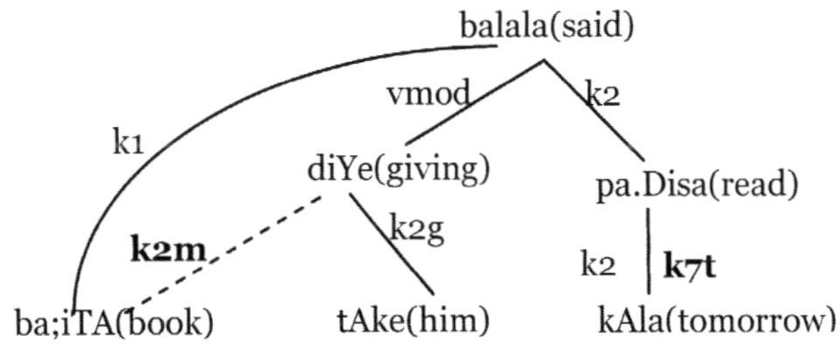

FIGURE 1 – Dependency tree for Example 1.

The corresponding dependency tree for Example 1 is shown in Figure 1. According to the transformed demand frame of the verb বলল (balala) [said] the Subject (k1) of this verb must be an animate noun. Therefore, the noun বইটা (ba;iTA) [book] can't be its Subject (k1). Then, according to the demand frame of the nearest verb দিয়ে (diYe) [giving] of this noun its Direct Object (k2m) is usually an inanimate noun. Again, according to the transformed demand frame of the verb পড়িস (pa.Disa) [read] a temporal noun can't be the karma of that verb. The temporal noun can be Temporal Locative (k7t) of that verb. Accordingly, we changed the attachments and relations given by the data driven parser.

2.1 আগামীকাল আমি কলকাতা যাব.
(AgAmikAla Ami kalakAtA yAba.)
[tomorrow I Kolkata will-go]
Tomorrow I will go to Kolkata.

2.2 গতকাল আমি কলকাতা দেখে এলাম.
(gatakAla Ami kalakAtA dekhe elAma.)
[yesterday I Kolkata see came]
Yesterday I visited Kolkata.

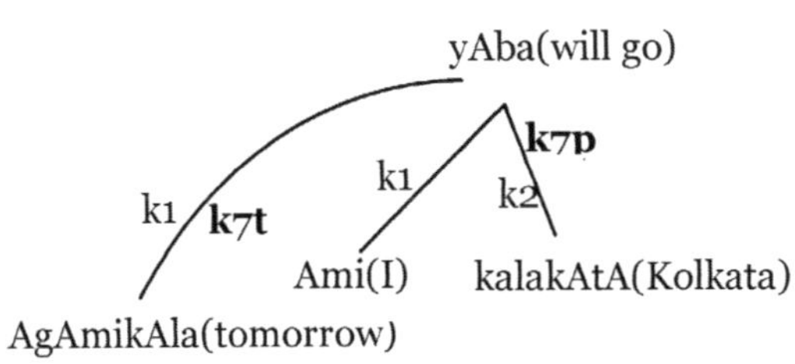

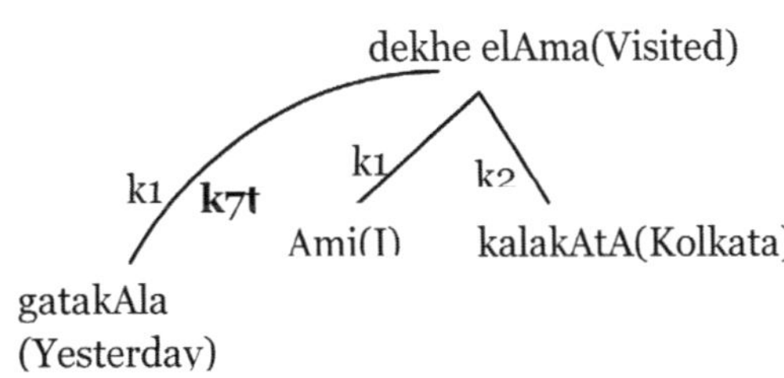

FIGURE 2(A) – Dependency tree for Example 2.1. FIGURE 2(B) – Dependency tree for Example 2.2.

The trees for Example 2.1 and Example 2.2 are shown in Figure 2(A) and 2(B), respectively. According to transformed demand frame of the verbs যাব (yAba) [will go] and দেখে_এলাম (dekhe elAma) [visited], a temporal noun can't be Subject (k1) of these verbs. This relation is changed to Temporal Locative (k7t). Again, according to the transformed demand frame of the verb যাবে (yAba) [will go], a spatial noun can't be Object (k2) and it is changed to Spatial Locative (k7p).

4 Evaluation Results

The data driven parser used in our task is trained on a Bangla Treebank containing 1200 sentences with an average length of 10.52 words. We tested the performance of this parser on a test data of 150 sentences.

In the grammar driven parser basic demand frames are prepared for 312 Bangla verbs and transformation rules for 12 Bangla verb features. Accuracy achieved by the data driven parser and the hybrid parser (data driven parser followed by grammar driven parser) are shown in Table 4. The table also contains the results achieved by other researchers for Bengali parsing on similar data-set. De et al. (2009) used a set of 500 Bangla demand frames and constraint based approach on the Bangla Treebank of ICON 2009. Kolachina et al. (2010) used MaltParser and various blended systems on the Bangla Treebank of ICON 2010.

	LAS	**UAS**	**LA**
Data Driven Parser	75.13	89.18	78.46
Hybrid Parser	80.35	89.63	84.20
De et al.	79.81	90.32	81.27
Kolachina et al.	75.65	88.14	78.67

TABLE 4 – Parser Evaluation Results.
LAS: Label Attachment Score, UAS: Unlabeled Attachment Score, LA: Label Accuracy.

The main improvements are achieved in the relations Subject (k1), Object (k2), Locative (k7) and Relation (r6). Table 5 shows the changes on the precision and recall of the label attachment scores of these relations.

	Subject		**Object**		**Locative**		**Relation**	
	R	P	R	P	R	P	R	P
Data Driven Parser	75.30	69.83	71.76	65.28	68.75	71.96	85.37	85.37
Hybrid Parser	86.06	83.04	82.44	78.83	77.27	73.91	89.02	83.91

TABLE 5 – Recall (R) and Precision (P) of subject, object, locative, and relation.

5 Conclusion

A two stage hybrid framework for dependency parsing of Bangla sentences is presented in this paper. In the first stage a data driven Bangla parser is developed using the experimentally calculated optimal features. We have developed a set of rules (called demand frames) for Bangla verbs. In the second stage, this demand frame based parser rectifies the mistakes in identifying the relations by the data driven parser.

More Bangla specific grammar rules may be developed for better performance of this framework. The performance of this framework can be tested for the parsing of sentences of other Indian language.

Acknowledgement

This work is partially supported by the ILMT project sponsored by TDIL program of MCIT, Govt. of India. We would like to thank all the members in Communication Empowerment Lab, IIT Kharagpur.

References

Begum, R., Husain, S., Bai, L., and Sharma, D. M. (2008). *Developing Verb Frames for Hindi*, In Proceedings LREC 2008.

Bharati, A., and Sangal, R. (1993). *Parsing Free Word Order Languages in the Paninian Framework*. In Proceedings of ACL:93.

Bharati, A., Sangal, R., and Reddy, T. P. (2002). *A Constraint Based Parser Using Integer Programming*. In Proceedings of ICON-2002.

Bharati, A., Husain, S., Vijay, M., Deepak, K., Sharma, D. M., and Sangal, R. (2009). *Constraint Based Hybrid Approach to Parsing Indian Languages*. In Proceedings of the 23rd Pacific Asia Conference on Language, Information and Computation (PACLIC 23), Hong Kong.

Chatterji, S., Sonare, P., Sarkar, S., and Roy, D. (2009). *Grammar Driven Rules for Hybrid Bengali Dependency Parsing*. In Proceedings of ICON09 NLP Tools Contest: Indian Language Dependency Parsing, Hyderabad, India.

De, S., Dhar, A., and Garain, U. (2009a). *Karaka Frames and Their Transformations for Bangla Verbs*. In 31st All-India Conference of Linguists, Hyderabad, India.

De, S., Dhar, A., and Garain, U. (2009b). *Structure Simplification and Demand Satisfaction Approach toDependency Parsing in Bangla*. In Proceedings of ICON09 NLP Tools Contest: Indian Language Dependency Parsing, Hyderabad, India.

Gadde, P., Jindal, K., Husain, S., Sharma, D.M., Sangal, R. (2010). *Improving Data Driven Dependency Parsing using Clausal Information*. Human Language Technologies: The 2010 Annual Conference of the North American Chapter of the ACL, pages 657–660, Los Angeles, California.

Ghosh, A., Das, A., Bhaskar, P. and Bandyopadhyay, S. (2010). Bengali Parsing System at ICON NLP Tool Contest 2010. In Proc of ICON-2010 tools contest on Indian language dependency parsing. Kharagpur, India.

Husain, S., Gadde, P., Ambati, B. R., Sharma, D., Sangal, R. (2009a). *A Modular Cascaded Approach to Complete Parsing*. IALP 2009, pages 141-146.

Husain, S. (2009b). *Dependency Parsers for Indian Languages*. In Proceedings of ICON09 NLP Tools Contest: Indian Language Dependency Parsing, Hyderabad, India.

Husain, S., Mannem, P., Ambati, B., and Gadde, P. (2010) *The ICON-2010 Tools Contest on Indian Language Dependency Parsing*. In Proceedings of ICON-2010 Tools Contest on Indian Language Dependency Parsing, Kharagpur, India.

Husain, S., Gadde, P., Nivre, J., Sangal, R. (2011). *Clausal parsing helps data-driven dependency parsing: Experiments with Hindi*. In Proceedings of IJCNLP 2011.

Kolachina, S., Kolachina, P., Agarwal, M., and Husain, S. (2010).*Experiments with MaltParser for parsingIndian Languages*. In Proc of *ICON-2010 tools contest on Indian language dependency parsing*. Kharagpur, India.

Mcdonald, R. (2007). *Characterizing the errors of data-driven dependency parsing models*. In Proceedings of the Conference on Empirical Methods in Natural Language Processing and Natural Language Learning.

Nivre, J., Hall, J., and Nilsson J. (2006). *MaltParser: A Data-Driven Parser-Generator for Dependency Parsing*. In Proceedings of the fifth international conference on Language Resources and Evaluation (LREC2006), Genoa, Italy, pages 2216-2219.

Nivre, J., Hall, J., Nilsson, J., Chanev, A., Eryigit, G., Kübler, S., Marinov S., and Marsi, E. (2007). *MaltParser: A language-independent system for data-driven dependency parsing*. Natural Language Engineering, 13(2), pages 95-135.

Nivre, J. (2009). *Parsing Indian Languages with MaltParser*. In Proceedings of ICON09 NLP Tools Contest: Indian Language Dependency Parsing, Hyderabad, India.

Repairing Bengali Verb Chunks for Improved Bengali to Hindi Machine Translation

Sanjay Chatterji, Nabanita Datta, Arnab Dhar, Biswanath Barik, Sudeshna Sarkar, Anupam Basu
Department of Computer Sc. & Engineering, Indian Institute of Technology, Kharagpur, India
Email:schatt@cse.iitkgp.ernet.in,nabanita.2121@gmail.com,{arnabdhar,bbarik,sudeshna,anupam}@cse.iitkgp.ernet.in

ABSTRACT

The present paper identifies the mistakes made by a data driven Bengali chunker. The analysis of a chunk based machine translation output shows that the major classes of errors are generated from the verb chunk identification mistakes. Therefore, based on the analysis of the types of mistakes in the Bengali verb chunk identification we propose some modules. These modules use tables of manually created entries which are validated using chunk annotated and dependency annotated corpus. These modules are used to repair the Bengali verb chunks and subsequently to improve the quality of Bengali to Hindi transfer based machine translation system.

1 Introduction

Bengali is a verb ending language (in general). The features of a Bengali finite verb include tense, aspect, mood, person, emphasizer, and voice. Similarly, Hindi is also a verb ending language (in general) and the features of a Hindi finite verb include tense, aspect, mood, gender, number, person, emphasizer, and voice.

In a Bengali to Hindi chunk based machine translation system the chunk tags and chunk boundaries of the Bengali input sentence are identified by a baseline data driven chunker with the help of a model built from a manually annotated training data. We have annotated 9000 Bengali sentences (250K words) manually using a chunk tagset containing 11 tags. This baseline data driven Bengali chunker often makes mistakes in identifying chunk boundaries and chunk tags. These mistakes subsequently give rise to errors in chunk based Bengali to Hindi machine translation system. Specifically, the mistakes in the verb chunks are the source of a major class of translation errors.

This paper works to improve the tags and boundaries of the Bengali verb chunks returned by the data driven chunker in order to improve the machine translation quality. As a preprocessing stage, a large Bengali corpus is annotated by this data driven chunker. We analyze the output of this chunker to formulate the rules to correct the misidentifications of the Bengali verb chunks and created some tables required to implement the rules. This data driven baseline chunker combined with the rule based modification can be considered as a hybrid chunker. We evaluate the performance of both the data driven and hybrid chunkers in terms of precision, recall and f-measure. We also evaluate the applications of the data driven and the hybrid Bengali chunkers in a transfer based Bengali to Hindi machine translation system in terms of BLEU and NIST scores.

2 Related Work

Pal and Bandyopadhyay (2012) have used aligned English and Bengali chunks to improve the performance of the English-Bengali Phrase Based Statistical Machine Translation System (PB-SMT). They have aligned English chunks with Bengali chunks automatically by validating the translations of English chunks with the original Bengali chunks. Only for the case of verb chunk alignment they were able to compare the translations of English verb chunks with the Bengali verb chunks as verb chunks have one-to-one correspondence in the English and Bengali chunk annotated sentences.

The nature of formation of different kinds of Bengali chunks are described by Das et al. (2005) and implemented by Das and Choudhury (2004). They have used the features of the arguments and predicates of the verbs to identify different chunks.

Due to unavailability of adequate training data, chunking for Bengali language has been attempted in rule based techniques. Bandyopadhyay and Ekbal (2006) have used some handcrafted Bengali specific rules to identify Bengali chunk boundary. These rules help in checking whether two neighboring POS tags belong to same chunk. The chunk tags are assigned based on the POS tags of the member words.

The task of identifying the chunks in Hindi sentences using syntactic rules has been carried out by Bharati et al. (1995) and using rewrite rules by Ray et al. (2003). Vilain and Day (2000) have used the transformation rules in the identification of the chunk tags from the POS tags.

Language specific rules are used to improve the performance of the data driven chunkers in hybrid framework by Bhat and Sharma (2011) for languages like Hindi, Kasmiri, etc. Bengali specific rules can also be used as a postprocessor with the data driven Bengali chunker of Dandapat (2007).

3 Our Work

3.1 Types of Chunks

As a preprocessing stage we have used a manually chunk annotated 9000 sentences (250k words) Bengali corpus to train a statistical model. This training data contains some top level chunk tags namely, noun chunk, verb chunk, adjectival chunk, adverbial chunk, conjuncts, etc.

We tag four types of Bengali verb chunks.

- Finite Verb Group (VGF) is used to indicate the features (tense, aspect, etc.) of the action of the corresponding clause.
- Non-Finite Verb Group (VGNF) is used to indicate intermediate action of the clause.
- Infinite Verb Group (VGINF) is used to mark infinitival (-te ending) verb forms.
- Gerundial Verb Group (VGNN) is used to mark gerundial (-A ending) verb forms.

These Bengali verb chunks have two parts.

- Main Verb (VM) is the compulsory part and is the main meaning bearing component of the verb chunk.
  - Sometimes, a single (finite or nonfinite) verb is used as VM. In the Bengali VGF বলে ফেলেছি (bale phelechhi) [have told] the nonfinite verb বলে (bale) [tell] acts as VM and in the Bengali VGF বলেছি (balechhi) [told] the finite verb বলেছি (balechhi) [told] acts as VM.
  - Sometimes, a complex predicate is used as VM. চোখে পড়া (chokhe pa.DA) [see] is an example Bengali complex predicate where the noun চোখে (chokhe) [eye] is related to the verb পড়া (pa.DA) [fall] by part-of dependency relation.
- A verb chunk may optionally contain a sequence of Auxiliary Verbs (VAUX) that follow the VM part. This sequence contains a sequence of nonfinite verbs followed by a finite verb. In the Bengali VGF বলে ফেলেছি (bale phelechhi) [have told] the finite verb ফেলেছি (phelechhi) [had] acts as VAUX.

3.2 Data Driven Chunker

We have implemented a data driven chunker that takes this 9000 sentence training data to build the model by implementing Conditional Random Field (CRF) of Lafferty et al. (2001) using the following feature set.

1. Word Features: Wi-2, Wi-1, Wi, Wi+1, Wi+2, (Wi-1, Wi), (Wi, Wi+1), (Wi-1, Wi, Wi+1).
2. POS And Chunk Features: POSi-2, POSi-1, POSi, POSi+1, CHUNKi-1.
3. Morphological features: MORi, Di, ABBi, LENGTHi, UNKi

In this feature set 'i' is the current position. The names of the attributes are given below.

- W – The Word
- POS – The Part-Of-Speech of the word
- CHUNK – The chunk tag of the word
- MOR – The morphological features and the suffix of the word
- D –Whether the word is a digit or not
- ABB – Whether the word is an abbreviation or not
- LENGTH – Whether the length of the word (number of characters) is greater than 4 or not
- UNK – Whether the word is an unknown word or not

This model is used to test 200 Bengali sentences. The Precision, Recall and F-measure of this data driven chunker on these test sentences are found to be 93.16, 86.64 and 89.78, respectively.

3.3 Analysis of mistakes of the data driven chunker

After analyzing the output of the data driven chunker we found that there are many errors. When we apply this data driven chunker to machine translation we found that some of these mistakes lead to errors in translation. As a post-processing step we are preparing rules to correct the Bengali verb chunks which affect the machine translation.

The types of mistakes in the identification of different types of Bengali verb chunks by this data driven chunker are discussed below. Based on the analysis we have categorized the verb chunk mistakes as follows.

1. Sometimes, the noun part of the complex predicate is kept outside the verb chunk by the data driven chunker. Again, the noun preceded by a verb chunk which is not the part of the complex predicate are kept inside the chunk. These kinds of mistakes are referred to as complex predicate related errors.

   In the Bengali phrase মনে করো এটা ভালো (mane karo eTA bhAlo) [suppose this is good] the complex predicate মনে করো (mane karo) [suppose] is broken into two parts মনে (mane)[in-mind] and করো (karo) [do] by the data driven chunker. Subsequently the Bengali phrase is translated to the wrong Hindi phrase मन में करो यह अच्छा है (mana me.N karo yaha achchhA hai).

2. Sometimes, the data driven chunker breaks a verb chunk into two chunks and sometimes it is added with the surrounding verbs to make a single chunk. These kinds of mistakes are referred to as compound verb related errors.

   In the Bengali phrase সে পেনটা বলে ফেলল (se penaTA bale phelala) [he dropped the pen after saying] the VGF ফেলল (phelala)[dropped] is added with the previous verb বলে (bale)[saying] to make the VGF chunk বলে ফেলল (bale phelala) [said] by the data driven chunker. Subsequently the Bengali phrase is translated to the wrong Hindi phrase बह पेन बोल चूका (baha pena bola chukA).

3. Sometimes, the data driven chunker tags some non-finite verbs in the VGNF chunks as finite verbs and sometimes as postpositions. In Bengali the nonfinite verbs of the form *a*e (bale, kare, dhare, etc.) are also used as finite verb. Similarly, the Bengali postpositions which are derived from verb root are also used as nonfinite verbs. These are referred to as VGNF related errors.

   In the Bengali phrase কথাটা বলে চলে গেল (kathATA bale chale gela) [went after telling the words] the VGNF বলে (bale) [telling] is tagged as VGF by the data driven chunker. Subsequently the Bengali phrase is translated to the wrong Hindi phrase बात कहता है चला गया (bAta kahatA hai chalA gayA).

3.4 Handling mistakes of the data driven chunker

Based on observation of mistakes of the Bengali baseline data driven chunker we build the following list based modules to correct them.

3.4.1 Module of handling complex predicate related errors

The baseline transfer based Bengali to Hindi machine translation system translates the noun part of the complex predicate separately. We have prepared a list of Bengali complex predicates and their translations in Hindi. This parallel Bengali Hindi complex predicate list is used to solve the complex predicate related errors.

However, some of the complex predicates can be translated by translating noun part and verb part separately. Sometimes, this approach of translation leads to incorrect translations. Some of the Bengali complex predicates which needs to be translated as a whole and their translation in Hindi and English are listed in Table1.

Bengali Complex Predicate	**Hindi Translation**	**English Translation**
রোপন করা (ropana karA)	रोपना (ropanA)	Transplant
আঘাত লাগা (AghAta lAgA)	लगना (laganA)	Embark
সেলাই করা (selAi karA)	सिलना (silanA)	Stitch
মনে হওয়া (mane haoYA)	लगना (laganA)	Seem
খিটখিট করা (khiTakhiTa karA)	टोकना (TokanA)	Punctuate
কাজে লাগা (kAje lAgA)	काम आना (kAma AnA)	Inure

TABLE 1 – Examples of Bengali complex predicates whose word by word translations lead to incorrect translations.

3.4.2 Module of handling unique representations

Some (verb, verb) pairs always have unique representations independent of the context. We make lists of such pairs for each type of representation. If the current (verb, verb) sequence exists in a list then the rule says that the sequence is represented in the corresponding way. Some of the examples of Bengali (verb, verb) pairs and their unique representations are listed in Table 2.

VM VAUX	PSP VM	VM VM
মরে যাওয়া (mare yAoYA)	দিয়ে হওয়া (diYe haoYA)	গিয়ে দেখা (giYe dekhA)
পাওয়া যাওয়া (pAoYA yAoYA)	থেকে চলা (theke chala)	আসতে চাওয়া (Asate chAoYA)
আছড়ে পড়া (Achha.De pa.DA)		আটকে রাখা (ATake rAkhA)

TABLE 2 – Examples of Bengali (verb, verb) pairs with unique representations

3.4.3 Module of handling ambiguous representations

In a sentence when a (verb, verb) pair is represented as (VM, VM), then these two verbs are in two different chunks. In the (VM, VAUX) representation, the pair is in a single chunk. Similarly, if the first verb of the (verb, verb) pair be represented as PSP and the second verb as VM, then these two words are in two different chunks. To resolve these conflicts, we enlist the ambiguous verbs along with the features of their dependents. This list is referred to as the demand frames of the verbs. Demand frame of a verb enlists the features of its dependents in a tabular form.

In this list we have also stored the features of the nouns with whom the verb may be attached as postposition. For instance, the থেকে (theke) postposition may co-occur with the noun which has 'র' (ra) or '0' (Zero) suffix in the singular number. So, an entry in this list is "থেকে র|0" (theke ra|Zero). In a Bengali corpus with 20,000 sentences, there are 103 different postpositions, out of which 11 are generated from verb root. These verb rooted postpositions are also used as non-finite verbs. These postpositions cum verbs are করে (kare), পরে (pare), ধরে (dhare), হয়ে (haYe), ছাড়া (chhA.DA), হতে (hate), নিয়ে (niYe), দিয়ে (diYe), থেকে (theke), ভাবে (bhAbe) and চেয়ে (cheYe).

This manually created list is validated by finding the entries in the Bengali Treebank. The features of the dependents of the verbs in the list are compared with features of its dependents in the Bengali Treebank. Similarly, the features of the noun with whom a verb may act as postposition as described in the list are compared with features of the noun with whom this verb acted as postposition in the Treebank.

If the current (verb, verb) sequence and the features of the associated dependents exist in the list then the rule says that the sequence belongs to the corresponding representation.

3.4.4 Module of identifying misidentification of auxiliary verb POS tag

A list of Bengali auxiliary verbs is created manually. If the second verb of the (verb, verb) sequence is there in that list then this sequence may be used as a single chunk otherwise not. The same list is also used for checking the validity of the first verb as auxiliary verb. Examples of Bengali auxiliary verb roots are হওয়া (haoYA) [to be], চলা (chalA) [go], থাকা (thAkA) [remain], etc.

4 Evaluation

We have taken 13199 Bengali sentences for formulating the proposed rules. As a preprocessing stage, we have executed Bengali morphological analyzer and Bengali Part-of-Speech tagger on these sentences. The rules are formulated based on the mistakes in the statistical chunking of these sentences.

4.1 Evaluating the performance of chunking

To test the performance of the proposed rules in correcting the chunks we have used 200 Bengali sentences from another distribution. The chunk tags and chunk boundaries in these test sentences given by the baseline data driven chunker are modified using the proposed modules in a sequential process. Amount of corrections of mistakes by each of these modules are given below.

The list of Bengali complex predicates contains 1063 entries. This list identified 135 complex predicates in these test sentences. Module for handling complex predicate related errors improved the chunking of 32 complex predicates.

The list of Bengali (verb, verb) pairs which have unique representations contains 211 entries. Using this list, module for handling unique representations identified 12 wrongly interpreted (verb, verb) pairs in these test sentences and corrected the respective chunks.

We have used demand frames for 312 Bengali verbs and for 11 Bengali post-positions. The module for handling ambiguous representations has improved the 21 chunks using these demand frames.

The list of 24 Bengali auxiliary verbs has been used in the module for identifying misidentification of auxiliary verbs by the POS tagger to improve 6 chunks.

The number of entries in each list and the number of chunk corrections in the test sentences are shown in Table 3. The performance of the data driven chunker and the hybrid chunker (data driven chunker followed by modules) are shown in Table 4 in terms of precision, recall and f-measure.

Name of the list	**Number of entries**	**Number of corrections**
Complex Predicate	1063	32
Unique	211	12
Demand Frame	312+11	21
Auxiliary Verb	24	6

TABLE 3 – The lists with number of entries and the corresponding number of corrections

	Precision	**Recall**	**F-measure**
Data Driven Chunker	93.16	86.64	89.78
Hybrid Chunker	93.42	88.02	90.64

Table 4 – Performance of data driven and hybrid chunkers

4.2 Evaluating the application of chunk modification modules in Machine Translation

Both the data driven chunker and the hybrid chunker are integrated into the Bengali to Hindi transfer based machine translation system. The translation system with the data driven chunker and that with the hybrid chunker show the effect of the proposed modules in the automatic translation of the Bengali sentences to Hindi.

Some of the example sentences with the chunk boundaries and chunk tags assigned by the baseline chunker and modified by the proposed rule based system are shown below. Their corresponding Hindi translations are also shown. In these examples the chunk tags and boundaries of the Bengali sentences given by both the baseline and hybrid systems are shown in Hindi outputs using Angle Brackets (<>) and Underscores (_), respectively.

1. Bengali Input (BI): এখানে আমরা নকশাখচিত শিবলিঙ্গ দেখলাম, আর ঘুরে বেড়ালাম পুরো মন্দির এলাকা । (ekhAne AmarA nakashAkhachita shibali~Nga dekhalAma, Ara ghure be.DAlAma puro mandira elAkA.)

   Baseline Output (BO): यहाँ हम नकशाखचित शिवलिंग देखे, और <घूमके>_VGNF <घुमा>_VGF पूरा मंदिर इलाका । (yahA.N hama nakashAkhachita shibali.nga dekhe, aura ghumake ghumA purA ma.ndira ilAkA.)

   Modified Output (MO): यहाँ हम नकशाखचित शिवलिंग देखे, और <घूम लिया>_VGF पूरा मंदिर इलाका । (yahA.N hama nakashAkhachita shibali.nga dekhe, aura ghuma liyA purA ma.ndira ilAkA.)

   Analysis: This is corrected using the rule that the word pair (ঘুরে বেড়ানো) should be a complex predicate as discussed in the module for handling complex predicate related errors.

2. BI: আমরা দোলমঞ্চ ঘুরে দেখে রাজবাড়ি থেকে বেরোলাম. (AmarA dolama~ncha ghure dekhe rAjabA.Di theke berolAma.)

   BO: हम दोलमंच <घूमके>_VGNF <देखके>_VGNF राजमहल <रहके निकला>_VGF। (hama dolama.ncha ghumake dekhake rAjamahala rahake nikalA.)

   MO: हम दोलमंच <घूमके>_VGNF <राजमहल से>_NP <निकला>_VGF। (hama dolama.ncha ghumake dekhake rAjamahala se nikalA .)

   Analysis: This is corrected using the rule that the (verb, verb) pair থেকে বেরোলাম (theke berolAma) can only be used as (PSP, VM). So, it is stored in the unique list as discussed in the module for handling unique representations.

3. Bengali Input (BI): অনেক কিছু দেখা হয়ে গেল । (aneka kichhu dekhA haYe gela.)

   Baseline Output (BO): बहत कुछ <देखना >_NP <हो गया>_VGF । (bahata kuchha dekhanA ho gaYA.)

   Modified Output (MO): बहत कुछ <देख लिया>_VGF । (bahata kuchha dekha liyA.)

   Analysis: This is corrected using the rule that the verb দেখা হওয়া (dekhA haoYA) with the karma (object) অনেক কিছু (aneka kichhu) should be considered as a single chunk as discussed in the module for handling ambiguous representations.

4. BI: চমত্কার কারুকার্যময় পুকুরঘাট পেছনে ফেলে দাঁড়িয়ে মন্দিরটি। (chamatkAra kArukAryamaYa pukuraghATa pechhane phele dA.N.DiYe mandiraTi.)

   BO: ख़ूबसूरत कारुकार्यमय तालाब घाट <पीछे>_NP <गिराके खरा है>_VGF मंदिर । (KUbasUrata kArukAryamaya tAlAba ghATa pIchhe girAke kharA hai ma.ndira.)

MO: ख़ूबसूरत कारुकार्यमय तालाब घाट <पीछे छोरके>_VGNF <खरा है>_VGF मंदिर । (KUbasUrata kArukAryamaya tAlAba ghATa pIchhe chhorake kharA hai ma.ndira.)

Analysis: This is corrected using the rule that the verb দাঁড়িয়ে (dA.N.DiYe) can't be used as VAUX. Therefore, they must be in two different chunks. This rule is discussed in the module for identifying misidentification of auxiliary verbs.

The BLEU and NIST scores of the translations of 180 sentences in these baseline and modified MT systems are shown in Table 4.

	BLEU	**NIST**
Baseline MT system	0.0988	3.3288
Modified MT system	0.1085	3.5087

TABLE 5 – BLEU and NIST scores of the Baseline and Modified MT systems

5 Conclusion

The chunk correction modules prepared for Bengali language can be adopted for similar other Indian languages, like Hindi. The lists required for these modules are easy to formulate. Whenever a mistake is found in the chunking then this can be resolved instantly by inserting some entry in these lists.

More modules may be developed by observing more data. These enhanced modules may also improve the performance of the chunking. However, more modules will also reduce the efficiency of the chunking.

Acknowledgement

This work is partially supported by the ILMT project sponsored by TDIL program of MCIT, Govt. of India. We would like to thank all the members in Communication Empowerment Lab, IIT Kharagpur for their active participation in developing the resources required for this work.

Reference

Bandyopadhyay, S. and Ekbal, A. (2006). *HMM Based POS Tagger and Rule-Based Chunker for Bengali.* In Proceedings of the Sixth International Conference on Advances In Pattern Recognition: pp. 384-390, Kolkata.

Bhat, R. A., and Sharma, D. M. (2011). *A Hybrid Approach to Kashmiri Shallow Parsing.* In LTC-2011: The 5th Language and Technology Conference: Human Language Technologies as a Challenge for Computer Science and Linguistics (LTC-2011).

Bharati, A., Chaitanya, V., and Sangal, R. (1995). *Natural Language Processing: A Paninian Perspective.* Prentice Hall India.

Dandapat, S. (2007) *Part Of Speech Tagging and Chunking with Maximum Entropy Model.* In Proceedings of IJCAI Workshop on "Shallow Parsing for South Asian Languages", Hyderabad, India. pp 29–32.

Das, D., Choudhury, M., Sarkar, S., and Basu, A. (2005). *An Affinity Based Greedy Approach towards Chunking for Indian Languages.* In Proceedings of ICON 2005 (NLP Association of India)

Das, D., and Choudhury, M. (2004). *Chunker and Shallow Parser for Free Word Order Languages: An Approach based on Valency Theory and Feature Structures.* Presented at the student paper competition of ICON 2004 (NLP Association of India).

Pal, S., and Bandyopadhyay, S. (2012). *Bootstrapping Method for Chunk Alignment in Phrase Based SMT.* In the Proceedings of the Joint workshop on exploiting Synergiesbetween Information Retieval and Machine Translation (ESIRMT) and Hybrid Approches to Machine Translation (HyTra), EACL-2012, pp.93-100, Avignon France.

Ray, P. R., Harish, V., Sarkar, S., and Basu A. (2003). *Part of Speech Tagging and Local Word Grouping Techniques for Natural Language Parsing in Hindi.* In Proceedings of International Conference on Natural Language Processing (ICON 2003). Mysore, India.

Vilain, M., and Day, D. (2000). *Phrase Parsing with Rule Sequence Processors: an Application to the Shared CoNLL Task.* In Proceedings of CoNLL-2000 and LLL-2000, Lisbon, Portugal.

De, S., Dhar, A., Biswas, S., and Garain, U. (2011). *On Development and Evaluation of a Chunker for Bangla.* In Proceedings of Second International Conference on Emerging Applications of Information Technology *(EAIT),* pp.321-324, 19-20 Feb.

Lafferty, J., McCallum, A., and Pereira, F. (2001). *Conditional Random Fields: Probabilistic Models for Segmenting and Labeling Sequence Data.* In *Proceedings of the Eighteenth International Conference on Machine Learning* (ICML-2001).

Domain Specific Ontology Extractor For Indian Languages

Brijesh Bhatt *Pushpak Bhattacharyya*
Center For Indian Language Technology, Indian Institute of Technology, Bombay
brijesh@cse.iitb.ac.in, pb@cse.iitb.ac.in

ABSTRACT
We present a k-partite graph learning algorithm for ontology extraction from unstructured text. The algorithm divides the initial set of terms into different partitions based on information content of the terms and then constructs ontology by detecting subsumption relation between terms in different partitions. This approach not only reduces the amount of computation required for ontology construction but also provides an additional level of term filtering. The experiments are conducted for Hindi and English and the performance is evaluated by comparing resulting ontology with manually constructed ontology for Health domain. We observe that our approach significantly improves the precision. The proposed approach does not require sophisticated NLP tools such as NER and parser and can be easily adopted for any language.

KEYWORDS: Ontology extraction, k-partite graph, wordnet, concept hierarchy.

1 Introduction

Ontology is defined as 'Explicit specification of conceptualization' (Gruber, 1993). As a knowledge representation formalism, ontologies have found a wide range of applications in the areas like knowledge management, information retrieval and information extraction.

As manual construction of ontology is a cumbersome task, many supervised and unsupervised techniques have been proposed to automatically construct ontology from the unstructured text. The ontology learning process involves two basic tasks- domain specific concept identification and constrution of concept hierarchy. Most of the existing algorithms extract relevant terms from the documents using various term extraction methods (Ahmad et al., 1999; Kozakov et al., 2004; Sclano and Velardi, 2007; Frantzi et al., 1998; Gacitua et al., 2011) and then construct ontology by identifying subsumption relations between terms.

Identifying top level concepts and creating a good concept hierarchy are the major challenges involved in the ontology learning tasks. As noted by Fountain and Lapata (2012), 'Most of the existing approaches construct flat structure rather than a taxonomy. Also, the automatically constructed ontologies often create false association between terms and result in erroneous concept hierarchy (Zhou, 2007).

In order to handle the above mentioned issues, we propose a graph-based ontology learning algorithm. Our approach is based on the information content of the term. 'Terms with high information content remain lower in the concept hierarchy and terms with low information content remain higher in the concept hierarchy' (Resnik, 1999). Caraballo and Charniak (1999) have shown that the term frequency is a good indicator of determining specificity of a term.

We divide the initial set of terms into different partitions based on the term frequency and then construct k-partite graph by finding subsumption relation between the terms of different partitions. This approach not just reduces the amount of computation required for ontology construction but also provides an additional level of term filtering. This early identification of hierarchy creates a better taxonomic structure and avoids false association between the terms.

The proposed approach combines evidences from linguistic patterns and WordNet (Fellbaum, 1998) to detect subsumption relation. The patterns used in the system are generic and can be used across languages. Wordnets of Indian languages are linked with each other and English WordNet through a common index (Bhattacharyya, 2010), which makes it possible to share concept definitions across languages.

Following are the major features of the proposed system:

- Ontology extraction process is completely unsupervised and does not require any human intervention.
- The lexical patterns used in the algorithm are generic and can work for any language.
- Proposed graph partition based algorithm not only requires less computation than the existing clustering techniques but also reduces false association between terms.
- The proposed system does not require sophisticated NLP techniques such as NER or parser and can be used for resource constrained languages.

The paper is organized as follows: section 2 describes related work, proposed algorithm is described in section 3 and section 4 discusses experiment and evaluation.

2 Related work

As noted by Leenheer and Moor (2005), 'No matter how expressive ontologies might be, they are all in fact lexical representations of concepts'. The linguistic basis of formal ontology is such that a significant portion of domain ontology can be extracted automatically from the domain related texts using language processing techniques. The problem of ontology learning is well studied for English. However, to the best of our knowledge no such efforts have been made so far for Indian languages.

Ontology learning approaches can be divided into three categories: heuristic based, statistical and hybrid techniques. Heuristic approach (Hearst, 1992; Berland and Charniak, 1999; Girju et al., 2003) primarily relies on the fact that ontological relations are typically expressed in language via a set of linguistic patterns. Hearst (1992) outlined a variety of lexico-syntactic patterns that can be used to find out ontological relations from a text. She described a syntagmatic technique for identifying hyponymy relations in free text by using frequently occurring patterns like '*NP0 such as NP1, NP2, . . . ,NPn*'. Berland and Charniak (1999) used a pattern-based approach to find out part-whole relationships (such as between car and door, or car and engine) in a text. Heuristic approaches rely on language-specific rules which cannot be transferred from one language to another.

Statistical approaches model ontology learning as a classification or clustering problem. Statistical methods relate concepts based on distributional hypothesis (Harris, 1968), that is 'similar terms appear in the similar context.' Hindle (1990) performed semantic clustering to find semantically similar nouns. They calculated the co-occurrence weight for each verb-subject and verb-object pair. Verb-wise similarity of two nouns is calculated as the minimum shared weight and the similarity of two nouns is the sum of all verb-wise similarities. Pereira et al. (1993) proposed a divisive clustering method to induce noun hierarchy from an encyclopedia.

Hybrid approaches leverage the strengths of both statistical and heuristic based approaches and often use evidences from existing knowledge bases such as wordnet, wikipedia, etc. Caraballo (1999) combined the lexico-syntactic patterns and distributional similarity based methods to construct ontology. Similarity between two nouns is calculated by computing the cosine between their respective vectors and used for hierarchical bottom-up clustering. Hearst-patterns are used to detect hypernymy relation between similar nouns. In a similar approach, Cimiano et al. (2005) clustered nouns based on distributional similarity and used Hearst-patterns, WordNet (Fellbaum, 1998) and patterns on the web as a hypernymy oracle for constructing a hierarchy. Unlike (Caraballo, 1999), the hypernymy sources are directly integrated into the clustering, deciding for each pair of nouns how they should be arranged into the hierarchy. Domínguez García et al. (2012) used wikipedia to extract ontology for different languages.

Like Cimiano et al. (2005), we follow a hybrid approach and construct a concept hierarchy using distributional similarity, patterns and WordNet. However, instead of performing top-down or bottom-up clustering, we pose ontology learning as a k-partite graph construction problem. We use term frequency to determine the position of a concept in the hierarchy. Ryu and Choi (2006) also used term frequency as a measure of domain specificity, but instead of partitioning they combined term frequency and distributional similarity to construct hierarchy. Other method similar to our work is proposed in Fountain and Lapata (2012). Fountain and Lapata (2012) proposed a graph based approach that does not require a separate term extraction step. However, their approach works with a predefined set of seed terms. Our approach is completely unsupervised and does not require any human intervention or predefined seed terms. Term frequency based partition provides early detection of the top level concepts and provides an additional level of term filtering.

3 Algorithm

The proposed algorithm poses ontology learning as a k-partite graph learning problem. The ontology graph is defined as a directed acyclic graph G(V, E), where V is a set of concept nodes and E is a set of relation edges. The proposed algorithm initially divides terms into different partitions and then constructs ontology by relating terms across partitions. The process involves three tasks, i.e., preprocessing, k-partite graph creation and concept hierarchy generation. Figure 1 represents the overall taxonomy learning process.

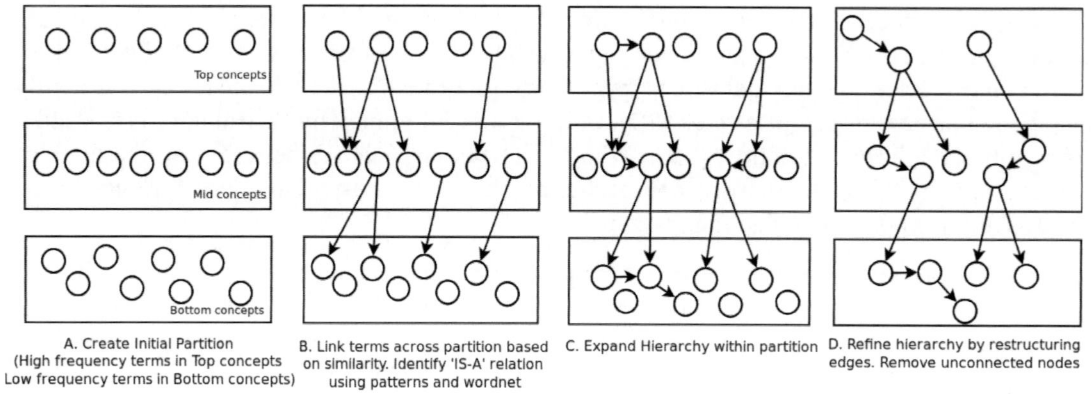

Figure 1: Taxonomy Learning Process

3.1 Preprocessing

This module extracts domain specific terms from the text corpus. The corpus is processed by performing morph analysis, POS tagging and stop word removal. Then lexical pattern $(NP) * (NP)$ is applied to extract key phrases from the corpus. Relevance of the key term in the corpus is calculated by counting the frequency of the term. Terms are filtered out using weirdness measure (Ahmad et al., 1999). Feature vector for each term is created by including co-occurring nouns, verbs and adjectives.

3.2 Initial Partition Creation

For each input term, concept node is created by calculating term frequency, feature vector and wordnet synsets. A concept node $v \in V$ is defined as $<t, tf, sid, v>$. where, t = lexeme for the concept, tf = Frequency of the term in corpus, sid = wordnet sense for the concept, v = feature vector for the concept. Once the concept nodes are created, the node set V is divided into three subsets based on frequency of the concept. High frequency terms are placed in top partition and low frequency terms are placed in bottom partition.

3.3 K-partite Graph Construction

This module constructs bipartite graph by finding relation edges between nodes of different partitions. The process involves two steps: calculate semantic relatedness between concepts and identify the type of relation i.e. subsumption.

As shown in algorithm 1, semantic relatedness between each concept pair (V_i, V_j), where $V_i \in C_i$ and $V_j \in C_j$, is measured by calculating cosine similarity between the feature vectors. The feature vector for a concept is constructed by including co-occurring nouns, verbs and adjectives. The weight of a feature is calculated using pointwise-mutual-information. A relation edge E(V_i , V_j) is created if the similarity value is found greater than the predefined threshold value.

Algorithm 1 *Link Partitions*

```
C_1 := concept nodes in Partition 1; m:= |C_1|
C_2 := concept nodes in Partition 2; n:= |C_2|
e := edge set; |e|:=0
for eachC_1i ∈ C_1andC_2j ∈ C_2 do
   similarity := (C⃗_1i ∩ C⃗_2j) / (|C_1i|*|C_2j|)
   if similarity > Threshold then
      create edge e_l := (C_1i, C_2j)
   end if
end for
```

Evidences from wordnet and lexico-syntactic patterns are used to detect name of the relation between semantically related concepts. Different relations identified during this phase are, subsumption (*e.g. pneumonia-disease*), neighbor (*e.g. malaria-pneumonia*) and similar (*e.g. procedure-process*).

Two patterns are used to detect *subsumption* and *neighbor* relations. Head word heuristic (Cimiano, 2006) based pattern $(NP)*(NP)$ is used to identify subsumption relation. As per head word heuristic $(NP1)(NP2)$ implies $(NP2)$ subsumes $(NP1NP2)$, *e.g. health-care program is-a-kind-of program*. This pattern often creates many false positives. False positives are reduced by applying frequency constraint; if $(NP1)(NP2)$ is in the low frequency partition and there exist term $(NP2)$ in high frequency partition then $(NP2)$ is parent of $(NP1)(NP2)$.

Various Hearst patterns to detect subsumption relation are, *'such NP as (NP,)∗ (and|or) NP'*, *'NP such as (NP,)∗ (and|or) NP'*, *'NP (, NP)∗ (,) or other NP'*, etc. Existing ontology extractors use many such patterns to detect subsumption relation. However, these patterns are specific to a language and in order to use the system for multiple languages we need to code these patterns for all languages. Instead, we generalize this to a single pattern, $((NP)*(NP)(and|or|,))*(NP)(NP)$. As per this pattern, if two or more noun phrases appear in the sentence separated by commas or conjunctions then these noun phrases are neighbors/co-hyponyms. For example, in a sentence *'such diseases as malaria and pneumonia....'* the original Hearst patterns can detect two subsumption relation edges (*malaria IS-A disease and pneumonia IS-A disease*), while our generalized pattern detects one neighbor/co-hyponymy relation (*malaria 'is neighbor' pneumonia*).

In addition to patterns, wordnet is also used to detect subsumption and synonymy relation between the terms. For the given pair of terms, synonymy is identified if they occur in the same synset for at least one sense pair. If the two terms are not synonyms, subsumption is investigated between the terms. If one term is the hypernymy of another, sense pair for which the hypernymy distance is smallest is returned as subsumption edge.

Algorithm 2 *Refine Hierarchy*

```
Graph(V, E)
while No change in edges do
  V := Concept Set; k:= |V|; E:= Edge Set; m:= |E|;
  for each E_i ∈ E do
    V_1 = source concept of E_i; V_2 = target concept of E_i
    if E_i is synonym then
      merge concept V_1 and V_2
    end if
    if E_i is neighbor then
      Create edges from parent of V_1 to V_2 and vice versa
    end if
  end for
  for each V_i ∈ V do
    V_p := parent of V_j; p := |V_p|;
    for each V_pq, V_pr ∈ V_p, V_pq ≠ V_pr do
      if V_pq is parent of V_pr then
        remove edge between V_pq and V_j
      end if
    end for
    V_c := children of V_j; p := |V_c|
    for each V_cq, V_cr ∈ V_c, V_cq ≠ V_cr do
      if V_cq is parent of V_cr then
        remove edge between V_j and V_pr
      end if
    end for
  end for
end while
```

3.4 Concept Hierarchy Creation

This process refines the k-partite graph constructed in the previous step and creates a concept hierarchy. A random walk through the nodes of the graph is performed to refine the relation hierarchy. Two major tasks performed during this phase are, (1) 'neighbor' and 'synonymy' edges constructed during previous phase are removed and new 'subsumption' edges are constructed accordingly. (2) The resulting subsumption graph is refined to improve hierarchy. Algorithm 2 describes the process.

During this process, the nodes linked with synonymy edge are merged and neighbor edges are removed. For each neighbor edge (V_i, V_j) subsumption edges are created from V_k to V_j, if V_k is parent of V_i and from V_l to V_i, if V_l is parent of V_j. The subsumption hierarchy is refined by investigating subsumption relation between each pair of concept for which there is a common subsuming node.

Finally, all concept nodes that do not have any incoming or outgoing edges are removed. 'k-partiteness' of the graph is ensured by checking that each weakly connected subgraph contains nodes from atleast two partitions. A weakly connected subgraph $G'(V', E')$ is removed if it does not contain at least one edge $e'(v_1, v_2) \in E'$ for which v_1 and v_2 are in different partition. This provides an additional level of term filtering and the relation edges which are not representative of the domain are removed.

4 Experiments and Observations

In order to evaluate performance of the system, we conducted our experiments on health corpus for two languages, Hindi and English. The details of the corpus is shown in table 1. We

Corpus	No. of Sentences	No. of Terms
English Health	15589	16498
Hindi Health	16002	14794

Table 1: corpus details

constructed ontology in both languages using our partitioned algorithm and without partition (similar to agglomerative clustering). We investigated relation across the layers to check which evidences are useful at which layer and compared the resulting ontology with a hand crafted ontology.

4.1 Layer wise evidence detection

Table 2 shows the source of evidence across layers. As shown in the table, in top partition the relation between concepts is detected more often using wordnet while in bottom partition evidences from lexico-syntactic patterns are more frequent. This is consistent with our hypothesis that top level concepts are general concepts and can be found in wordnets.

Partition	English Health		Hindi Health	
	LSP	WORDNET	LSP	WORDNET
Top	75	214	0	85
Mid	238	1012	23	313
Bottom	342	313	297	91
Mid-Bottom	420	1094	138	310
Top-Mid	137	1050	5	399
Top-Bottom	131	549	39	191

Table 2: Layer wise evidence

4.2 Comparison with gold standard

The quality of the ontology constructed is evaluated by comparing it with the hand crafted ontology. The lexical precision and recall is calculated using following formula,

Recall $= |c1 \bigcap c2|/c2$

Precision $= |c1 \bigcap c2|/c1$

where c1 is the set of concept in automatically constructed ontology and

c2 is the set of concepts in hand crafted gold standard.

Table 3 shows the precision and recall for both cases: with partition and without partition. As shown in table 3, the precision is higher for partitioned algorithm.

	Precision	Recall	F-Score
English-Health No Partition	0.69	0.83	0.75
English-Health Partition	0.75	0.7298	0.7298
Hindi-Health No Partition	0.81	0.604	0.6789
Hindi-Health Partition	0.9251	0.7679	0.8387

Table 3: Evaluation against hand crafted ontology

Conclusion

We have presented a novel graph based algorithm for domain specific ontology extraction. Our approach is unsupervised and does not require any human intervention. The proposed system can be easily adopted for any language. Using our algorithm, we constructed 'health domain ontology' from English and Hindi text corpora and the resulting ontology is compared against a manually constructed ontology. It is observed that partitioning improves the precision without sacrificing F-Score. We also observe that the high frequency terms remain at the top level in the ontology and definition for these terms are often found in wordnet, while lexico-syntactic patterns are found more often in low frequency terms. Our future aim is to include automatic extraction of non-taxonomic relations between concepts.

References

Ahmad, K., Gillam, L., Tostevin, L., and Group, A. (1999). Weirdness indexing for logical document extrapolation and retrieval (wilder). In *The Eighth Text REtrieval Conference*.

Berland, M. and Charniak, E. (1999). Finding parts in very large corpora. In *Proceedings of the 37th annual meeting of the Association for Computational Linguistics on Computational Linguistics*, ACL '99, pages 57–64, Stroudsburg, PA, USA. Association for Computational Linguistics.

Bhattacharyya, P. (2010). Indowordnet. In *Proceedings of the Seventh conference on International Language Resources and Evaluation (LREC'10)*.

Caraballo, S. A. (1999). Automatic construction of a hypernym-labeled noun hierarchy from text. In *Proceedings of the 37th annual meeting of the Association for Computational Linguistics*, pages 120–126.

Caraballo, S. A. and Charniak, E. (1999). Determining the specificity of nouns from text. In *Proceedings SIGDAT-99*, pages 63–70.

Cimiano, P. (2006). *Ontology Learning and Population from Text: Algorithms, Evaluation and Applications*. Springer-Verlag New York, Inc., Secaucus, NJ, USA.

Cimiano, P., Pivk, A., Schmidt-Thieme, L., and Staab, S. (2005). Learning taxonomic relations from heterogeneous sources of evidence. *Ontology Learning from Text: Methods, Evaluation and Applications*.

Domínguez García, R., Schmidt, S., Rensing, C., and Steinmetz, R. (2012). Automatic taxonomy extraction in different languages using wikipedia and minimal language-specific information. In *Proceedings of the 13th international conference on Computational Linguistics and Intelligent Text Processing - Part I*, CICLing'12, pages 42–53, Berlin, Heidelberg. Springer-Verlag.

Fellbaum, C. (1998). *WordNet: An Electronic Lexical Database*. Bradford Books.

Fountain, T. and Lapata, M. (2012). Taxonomy induction using hierarchical random graphs. In *Proceedings of the 2012 Conference of the North American Chapter of the Association for Computational Linguistics: Human Language Technologies*, pages 466–476, Montréal, Canada. Association for Computational Linguistics.

Frantzi, K. T., Ananiadou, S., and Tsujii, J.-i. (1998). The c-value/nc-value method of automatic recognition for multi-word terms. In *Proceedings of the Second European Conference on Research and Advanced Technology for Digital Libraries*, ECDL '98, pages 585–604, London, UK, UK. Springer-Verlag.

Gacitua, R., Sawyer, P., and Gervasi, V. (2011). Relevance-based abstraction identification: technique and evaluation. *Requir. Eng.*, 16(3):251–265.

Girju, R., Badulescu, A., and Moldovan, D. (2003). Learning semantic constraints for the automatic discovery of part-whole relations. In *Proceedings of HLT/NAACL-03*, pages 80–87.

Gruber, T. R. (1993). Towards principles for the design of ontologies used for knowledge sharing. In *Formal Ontology in Conceptual Analysis and Knowledge Representation*, Deventer, The Netherlands. Kluwer Academic Publishers.

Harris, Z. (1968). Mathematical structures of language. John Wiley Sons.

Hearst, M. A. (1992). Automatic acquisition of hyponyms from large text corpora. In *Proceedings of the 14th International Conference on Computational Linguistics*, pages 539–545.

Hindle, D. (1990). Noun classification from predicate-argument structures. In *Proceedings of the 28th annual meeting on Association for Computational Linguistics*, ACL '90, pages 268–275, Stroudsburg, PA, USA. Association for Computational Linguistics.

Kozakov, L., Park, Y., Fin, T.-H., Drissi, Y., Doganata, Y. N., and Cofino, T. (2004). Glossary extraction and utilization in the information search and delivery system for ibm technical support. *IBM Systems Journal*, 43(3):546–563.

Leenheer, P. D. and Moor, A. D. (2005). Context-driven disambiguation in ontology elicitation. In *Context and Ontologies: Theory, Practice, and Applications. Proc. of the 1st Context and Ontologies Workshop, AAAI/IAAI 2005*, pages 17–24. AAAI Press.

Pereira, F., Tishby, N., and Lee, L. (1993). Distributional clustering of english words. In *Proceedings of the 31st Annual Meeting of the Association for Computational Linguistics*, pages 183–190.

Resnik, P. (1999). Semantic similarity in a taxonomy: An information-based measure and its application to problems of ambiguity in natural language. *J. Artif. Intell. Res. (JAIR)*, 11:95–130.

Ryu, P.-M. and Choi (2006). Taxonomy learning using term specificity and similarity. In *Proceedings of the 2nd Workshop on Ontology Learning and Population: Bridging the Gap between Text and Knowledge*, pages 41–48, Sydney, Australia. Association for Computational Linguistics.

Sclano, F. and Velardi, P. (2007). Termextractor: a web application to learn the shared terminology of emergent web communities.

Zhou, L. (2007). Ontology learning: state of the art and open issues. *Information Technology and Management*, 8:241–252. 10.1007/s10799-007-0019-5.

Constrained Hidden Markov Model for Bilingual Keyword Pairs Alignment

Denny Cahyadi *Fabien Cromieres* *Sadao Kurohashi*
Graduate School of Informatics, Kyoto University
Yoshida-Honmachi, Sakyo-ku, Kyoto, 606-8501, Japan
{denny,fabien}@nlp.ist.i.kyoto-u.ac.jp, kuro@i.kyoto-u.ac.jp

Abstract

Bilingual terminology dictionaries are resources of much practical importance in many application of bilingual NLP. Because technical terminology can be both very specific and rapidly evolving, it can however be difficult to obtain dictionaries with good coverage. Mining automatically such terminology from technical documents is therefore an attractive possibility. With this goal in mind, and following some previous works, we devise an algorithm that is efficient at aligning the bilingual keyword list of scientific papers. Our results show that our approach can extract bilingual terms with very good precision and recall.

Keywords: Hidden Markov Model, lexicon extraction, word alignment, alignment model.

1 Introduction

Bilingual terminology dictionaries can be critically useful for many practical tasks such as Machine Translation of technical documents, cross-language Information Retrieval or simply as a resource to human translators. Bilingual dictionaries of technical terms with good coverage and quality can however be difficult to obtain, both due to the high domain-specificity of most technical terms and the continuous creation of new terms as new research is being conducted and new technics are being developed.

Because of this, some research has been done to extract automatically such bilingual dictionaries from technical documents. This paper will try to further this research, in particular by following a previously proposed idea of aligning the keywords list of technical and scientific documents.

We propose an approach to adapt existing word-alignment algorithm to the task of keyword-list alignment. This is done by enforcing constraints on the keyword boundaries and by using a different distortion model for the keywords and the words within each keyword. In particular, we show that our modified version of the HMM alignment algorithm of (Vogel et al., 1996) perform better than both the original HMM algorithm and the commonly used word-aligner GIZA++ for the keyword alignment task.

2 Related works

If one has a large amount of technical documents in the relevant domain that are written in the two languages of interest, one can of course extract bilingual term pairs by running one of the many word-alignment algorithm that have already been proposed (such as (Brown et al., 1993) or (Vogel et al., 1996)). However, such bilingual collection of documents are not easily obtained. Besides, the word-alignment algorithms will not by themselves indicate which set of words represent a technical term. We will focus here on approaches that do not require such large bilingual collection of technical documents.

(Lin et al., 2008) reported experiments of extracting term pairs from part of document which contains parentheses. It is based on the fact that the English translation of a technical term is sometimes written inside a parenthesis next to it. Their method involves building a kind of parallel corpus by extracting the English terms in parenthesis and the words appearing before the parentheses, filtering the non-translation words, and then aligning the English terms with an unsupervised word alignment method.

(Nagata et al., 2001) extracted term pairs not only from parentheses, but also from glossaries and parallel paragraph. In their works, term pairs are filtered out if they are unlikely translation of each other. The likeliness is calculated based on their locations. Foreign and English terms which are appearing close to each other are considered to have higher translation likeliness. Their work is focused on extracting technical term pairs from Japanese documents.

(Ren et al., 2010) extracted bilingual technical term pairs from keyword section of abstracts of Chinese research papers. In their method, Chinese and English keywords are aligned monotonically[1] based on their writing order if the lists contain the same number of keywords. Otherwise, a seed bilingual dictionary is used to detect partial translation.

[1]Here and in the following, a monotonic alignment is one in which the first source keyword is aligned with the first target keyword, the second source keyword with the second target one, etc.

キーワード: 有機半導体レーザ、有機発光ダイオード、分布帰還レーザ、屈折率回折格子
Keyword: organic semiconductor laser, distributed feedback, organic light-emitting diode, refractive index grating

Figure 1: An example of non-monotonic alignment. The second English keyword is a translation of third Japanese and the third English keyword is a partial translation of second Japanese keyword

Keywords which contain partial translation of each other are then aligned. Finally, keywords are filtered based on their inverse-domain score. This step is done to make sure that the keyword extracted are technical terms (not general term).

In this paper, we follow the idea of aligning keyword lists. However, instead of using a seed bilingual dictionary and making a strong assumption of monotonicity for the keyword order, we develop an unsupervised approach based on the adaptation of existing word-alignment algorithms to the specificities of the keyword-alignment task.

3 Keyword Alignment Model

3.1 Keyword Alignment Problem and Constraint

Figure 1 gives an example of the type of keyword list one can find in the description of a Japanese scientific paper. The keywords will often be written in the same order in both languages, but this is far from being systematic. Some keywords might also be mentioned in one language and not the other. For example, in our Japanese-English data (see section 4), around one third of the keyword lists exhibit different writing order or non-symmetric use of keywords.

The task of automatically aligning keyword lists presents some differences with the more common word-alignment of sentences. These differences can limit the efficiency of directly applying existing word alignment algorithm. Indeed, using such word-alignment algorithm lead to the question of what should be the elementary alignment unit (i.e. the "word" for the algorithm). It is natural to consider each individual word in the keyword list to be an alignment unit. But then, the alignment algorithm might produce alignments breaking the keyword boundaries: two words of the same source keywords might be aligned with two words in different target keywords. If on the other hand, one consider each keyword to be an alignment unit, data sparseness problem will appear: if "maximum entropy" is considered as a single unit, we cannot use the knowledge we may have of the translation of "maximum" or "entropy" to find the alignment.

An additional issue that will appear when using words as the alignment unit is that the order of the words in the keyword list is the result of two effects: the word order inside a keyword (that will follow the source or target language grammar), and the order of the keywords themselves (that will often -but not always- be similar between the source and target keyword list). Classic word-alignment algorithm are usually not designed to handle efficiently this kind of two-factor word distortion.

In the following, we will try to define an alignment model that address these issues. Many well-known word alignment algorithms ((Vogel et al., 1996), (Brown et al., 1993)) make use of a probabilistic distortion model that is estimating the probability of source and target words to be aligned depending on their position. We propose to augment these models with a 2-level distortion probability: a word-level distortion and a keyword-level distortion. This will serve two purpose: ensuring that the keyword boundaries are respected by the word-alignment, and modeling the two-factor word distortion.

We chose to focus on the HMM alignment model of (Vogel et al., 1996), as it is both simple (and thus easy to adapt) and efficient. However, the idea we develop here could be applied to most alignment model.

3.2 Standard HMM alignment

We briefly review the classic HMM alignment model of (Vogel et al., 1996). It is an asymmetric 1-to-n alignment model. e represents a source (or English) sentence, with e_i being the word at position i. Likewise, f is a target (or Foreign) sentence. The alignment variable a assign an English word (or a special Null word) to each foreign word: $a_i = j$ means that f_i is aligned with e_j. The probability of $P(a, f|e)$ is expressed as an HMM, where the hidden states are the source words e_j, the observed sequence is the target sentence f, and a specify a possible sequence of hidden states generating f:

$$P(a, f|e) = \prod_{j=1}^{|f|} P_{dist}(a_j|a_{j-1}) \cdot P_{trans}(f_j|e_{a_j}) \quad (1)$$

$P_{dist}(k|l)$, the state transition probability (or *distortion* probability), specify the probability of the alignment of two adjacent foreign words jumping from e_l to e_k. $P_{trans}(f_j|e_{a_j})$, the emission probability (or *translation* probability), specify the probability that f_j is the translation of e_{a_j}. This model can be trained on parallel sentences using the classic Baum-Welch algorithm.

3.3 Constrained HMM alignment

In the context of keyword lists, the position of a word is better represented as a pair of integer $i.j$, meaning that the word is at position j in keyword i. $a_{i.j} = k.l$ means that the source word at position $i.j$ is aligned with the target word at position $k.l$. Each keyword in both languages is augmented at the end with a special EOK (End of Keyword) word (we note $i.EOK$ the position of the EOK of keyword i). Each English keyword is also augmented with a special Null keyword.

We modify the HMM alignment model in order to solve the problems mentioned in section 3.1. We call this modified model *constrained HMM* since we enforce a constraint on the state transition so that every word alignment will respect the keyword boundaries. The constraint is expressed as the following: State transition to any arbitrary state is allowed only in the very beginning or after the aligner reach the end of a keyword (EOK) on the target side. In any other time, state transition is only allowed from the current state to another state that corresponds to the same keyword than the current state. In other words, we set $P_n(a_{j.n}|a_{i.m}) = 0$ if $m \neq EOK$ and $i \neq j$.

We decompose the state transition model into a keyword transition probability P_{distK} and a word transition probability P_{distW}. The initial probability of the first keyword and the first word of a keyword are given, respectively, by P_{initK} and P_{initW}.

The final state transition probability can then be expressed as follow (note the $j.n$ subscript of $P_{j.n}$ that shows that this transition probability will change depending on the position in a target keyword). :

$$P_{j.n}(a_{j.n} = k.l | a_{i.m} = k'.l') = \begin{cases} P_{initK}(k) \cdot P_{initW}(l) & \text{if } j = 1 \text{ and } n = 1 \\ P_{distK}(k|k') \cdot P_{initW}(l) & \text{if } n = 1 \\ P_{distW}(l|l') \cdot \delta_{kk'} & \text{otherwise} \end{cases} \tag{2}$$

In this formula, $\delta_{kk'}$ is a Kronecker delta (equal to 1 if $k = k'$, else 0). $i.m$ is always the position in the target keyword list just before $j.n$.

With this expression of the distortion, we have solved the issues we describes: the word alignment will respect keywords boundaries, and we model separately the keyword order and the word order inside the keywords. This lead to better alignment results, as we will see in section 4. The improvement can also be seen in the light of (Roweis, 2000), that shows that constraining a HMM in a way consistent with a task will lead to better a training. Note also that this model can be seen as aligning both words and keywords: although it gives a word alignment, the keyword boundary constraint means that this 1-to-n word alignment define unambiguously a 1-to-n keyword alignment.

3.4 Time-homogeneous implementation

This HMM model is not time homogeneous: the transition probability matrix is not the same depending on if we are in the middle or at the end of a target keyword. The Viterbi algorithm and the Baum-Welch training algorithm can perfectly be applied to such a HMM. However, many existing HMM library assume time homogeneity. If one want to use such library, it can be convenient to cast our model as a time-homogeneous HMM. This can be done at the price of doubling the number of states.

Firstly we want to know whether the current state corresponds to the same keyword than the previous state in the sequence. For this purpose, the number of hidden states is doubled. The originals are marked as e_i^{new} and their duplicates are marked as e_i^{cont}. State e_i^{new} is used if current state corresponds to different keyword than what the previous state corresponds to, otherwise e_i^{cont} is used.

By having these states, state sequence can be controlled easily by applying the following rules to the state transition model: 1) if current state is e_i^{new} then only transition to e_i^{cont} is allowed; 2) if current state is e_i^{cont}, then transition to any e_i^{cont} or EOK is allowed; 3) if current state is EOK, then only transition to e_i^{new} is allowed. For state emission model, the following rule are applied: visible state $f_{j.EOK}$ of foreign keyword f_j can only be emitted by hidden state $e_{i.EOK}$.

3.5 Variants

The natural way of finding the best alignment according to a trained HMM model is to use Viterbi decoding. However, (Liang et al., 2006) reports that one can get better results by computing the expected probability of each link and keeping those above a certain threshold. We can apply this idea here, although in our case we will want to use the expected probability of two keyword being aligned (easily computed from the expected probabilities of the word links).

Our HMM model is, like the original one, a 1-to-n alignment model. As is often done in such case, we can align each keyword list twice, with each language taken alternatively as the source language. We then combine the resulting alignments by intersecting their set of keyword links.

Although it is possible to start the training of the HMM model from some random model, it can also be beneficial to initialize the translation probabilities with those obtained from the simpler IBM Model 1 (Brown et al., 1993).

(Liang et al., 2006) show that it is beneficial for the final alignment quality to also train jointly the parameters of the HMM for each direction. We tried to do this, but did not observe any improvement in our results. We are not sure at this stage if this is due to the specificities of the task and the data, or to a subtle problem in our use of the training by agreement method.

Observing that more than half of all authors choose to write the keyword lists in both language in a perfectly parallel way (same keywords and same order), we also considered a model that would be a mixture of two HMM models: one such as the one we described in the previous section, and one that constrain the keyword order to be monotonic. We were thus hoping to model the idea that our data was actually generated by a mix of two sources: "organized" authors, that write perfectly parallel pairs of keywords lists, and "disorganized" authors, that take more freedom when they write these keyword lists. Unfortunately, this approach did not yield any improvement either. We are still unsure if the problem is with the basic assumptions or the way we designed and implemented the model.

Because the training by agreement and the mixture of model idea did not improve the results while complexifying the model and the implementation, we do not mention them in the experiment section.

4 Experiment

4.1 Data description

We conduct some experiments for extracting Japanese-English keyword pairs from Japanese research paper. We could obtain around 4 millions abstract of Japanese scientific papers, originating from CiNii[2] web portal. Only about 720k of them contain both English and Japanese keyword lists. We use these lists as the dataset for all experiments.

We create two sets of annotated keyword lists pairs to be used as test set and tuning set respectively. The main use of the tuning set is to set the threshold of alignment when we use the expected probability of each link instead of the Viterbi alignment (see section 3.5). Each set contains 100 keyword lists pairs taken randomly from the dataset. These pairs are aligned manually by two native Japanese speakers who are also fluent in English.

Segmentation for Japanese words is done using JUMAN (Kurohashi et al.). A keyword list usually contains about 2 to 20 keywords with average of 8 keywords. There are a total of 807 Japanese keywords in the test set.

[2] http://ci.nii.ac.jp

4.2 Baseline and Setup

Three different methods are used for baseline. As the first baseline, keywords are aligned monotonically in a way similar to (Ren et al., 2010) except we did not do the partial translation alignment as we want to consider unsupervised methods with no seed dictionary available. This baseline is called `mono-all` when we apply it to all keyword list, and `mono-same` when we apply it only to keyword list with the same length.

For the second baseline, alignment is done using GIZA++ alignment tool (Och and Ney, 2003) with its default setting. Alignment was done both way then merged by intersection[3]. With this method we conduct two experiments: using word (`wGIZA-i`) and keyword (`kGIZA-i`) as the alignment unit. When using word as the alignment unit, a keyword links is created for each word link. The `wGIZA-i` approach will tend to produce more links and possibly many-to-many keyword alignments, resulting in higher recall but lower precision than the `kGIZA-i` approach. For the third baseline, standard HMM (`sHMM`) is used for the alignment, with keyword as the alignment unit.

For the implementation of our constrained HMM, we conducted 4 experiments. First we applied constrained HMM in only one direction, with setup similar to `sHMM`, with and without initializing with the IBM Model1 parameters (`cHMM` and `cHMM-ibm`, see section 3.5). We then used bidirectional alignments using intersect method (`cHMM-ibm-i`).

Finally, we tried to create the alignment not by Viterbi decoding, but by thresholding the expected probability of the keyword links (`cHMM-ibm-i-t`, see section 3.5). Optimum threshold is determined using a separate tuning set.

4.3 Result

Method	Test set	Recall	Precision	F-score
`mono-same`	`test-set`	0.861	**0.968**	0.911
`mono-all`	`test-set`	0.890	0.742	0.809
`wGIZA-i`	`test-set`	0.970	0.867	0.915
`kGIZA-i`	`test-set`	0.922	0.906	0.914
`sHMM`	`test-set`	0.928	0.603	0.731
`cHMM`	`test-set`	0.968	0.629	0.763
`cHMM-ibm`	`test-set`	**0.977**	0.636	0.770
`cHMM-ibm-i`	`test-set`	0.956	0.898	0.926
`cHMM-ibm-i-t`	`test-set`	0.954	0.918	**0.936**
`mono-same`	`test-set-equal-length`	0.983	0.977	0.980
`cHMM-ibm-i-t`	`test-set-equal-length`	0.998	0.998	**0.998**

Table 1: Recall, Precision, and F-score of each method

The result of our experiments is shown in Table 1. They show several interesting things. One is that our modification to the HMM model yield improvement in both precision and recall over the standard version (`sHMM` vs `cHMM`). This appears to validate our view that modeling the specificities of the keywords lists is beneficial to alignment.

[3]The "grow-diag-final" heuristic is often used instead of a simple intersection. However, we found that in the case of keyword list, it was not performing better than a simple intersection.

Another interesting point is that the best version of our algorithm (`cHMM-ibm-i-t`) outperform all our baselines in term of F-measure by at least 2% absolute (corresponding to a relative error[4] reduction of 25%). It also gives the second best precision, behind the somewhat conservative heuristic `mono-same`. However, tuning the threshold used in `cHMM-ibm-i-t` for optimal precision rather than for optimal F-score would change that (see also section 4.4).

4.4 Closer comparison with the monotonic heuristics

Given the very good performance of `mono-same` and `mono-all` (with respect to their simplicity), we tried to compare the performance of our algorithm on the subset of data for which these heuristics should perform the best (and for which they are used in (Ren et al., 2010)): keyword lists with the same length.

We selected the 68 list pairs of our test set having the same number of English and Japanese keywords (`test-set-equal-length`). Of these, 63 are actually perfectly parallel keyword lists. The result (Table 1) shows that the monotonic heuristics are outperformed by our algorithm: it can not only detect all of the perfectly aligned pairs, but also correctly align 4 of the 5 non-monotonic lists.

4.5 Chinese-English

We intend to conduct a similar experiment for Chinese-English keyword list pairs. However we have so far only collected 70,000 such keyword lists. We report however our preliminary result on this smaller data set. Our alignment algorithm is still performing better than standard word-aligners such as Giza++ (by around 3.6% absolute F-score). However, it turns out that the simpler baseline of aligning monotonically each keywords (*mono-all*) gives even better results (2.4% absolute F-score difference) . This appears to be due to two reasons. One is that the smaller training data size has a negative impact on statistical aligners. The other is that there is much more perfectly parallel keyword lists in this dataset (more than 90%). The idea of a mixture of models (section 3.5) could therefore be effective on such data set.

Conclusion and perspectives

We considered the problem of aligning the bilingual keyword lists of scientific papers, with the goal of automatic bilingual terms extraction. We proposed to modify existing word-alignment algorithms in order to better take into account the specificities of this task. Our method show significant improvement over previous approaches and general word aligner, achieving better results than the often used Giza++ word aligner while having much less complexity. Besides the modifications we proposed could be applied to more complex alignment algorithm as well.

We need to investigate more, however, why some of our other tentative improvements (such as the training by agreement or the mixture of models) did not yield better results. We are also in the process of gathering additional Chinese-English data to perform more experiments in this language pair, and ultimately plan to combine and filter the two data sources to create a Japanese-Chinese dictionary of technical terms.

[4]Where we compute the error as 1 minus the F-score.

References

Brown, P. F., Pietra, V. J. D., Pietra, S. A. D., and Mercer, R. L. (1993). The mathematics of statistical machine translation: parameter estimation. *Comput. Linguist.*, 19(2):263–311.

Kurohashi, S., Nakamura, T., Matsumoto, Y., and Nagao, M. Improvements of japanese morphological analyzer JUMAN. In *Proceedings of the International Workshop on Sharable Natural Language*, pages 22–28.

Liang, P., Taskar, B., and Klein, D. (2006). Alignment by agreement. In *Proceedings of the main conference on Human Language Technology Conference of the North American Chapter of the Association of Computational Linguistics*, HLT-NAACL '06, pages 104–111, Stroudsburg, PA, USA. Association for Computational Linguistics.

Lin, D., Zhao, S., Durme, B. V., and Pasca, M. (2008). Mining parenthetical translations from the web by word alignment. In McKeown, K., Moore, J. D., Teufel, S., Allan, J., and Furui, S., editors, *ACL*, pages 994–1002. The Association for Computer Linguistics.

Nagata, M., Saito, T., and Suzuki, K. (2001). Using the web as a bilingual dictionary. In *Proceedings of the workshop on Data-driven methods in machine translation - Volume 14*, DMMT '01, pages 1–8, Stroudsburg, PA, USA. Association for Computational Linguistics.

Och, F. J. and Ney, H. (2003). A systematic comparison of various statistical alignment models. *Comput. Linguist.*, 29(1):19–51.

Ren, F., Zhu, J., and Wang, H. (2010). Web-based technical term translation pairs mining for patent document translation. In *Natural Language Processing and Knowledge Engineering (NLP-KE), 2010 International Conference on*, pages 1–8.

Roweis, S. (2000). Constrained hidden markov models. In *In Solla et al. (2000*, pages 782–788. MIT Press.

Vogel, S., Ney, H., and Tillmann, C. (1996). Hmm-based word alignment in statistical translation. In *Proceedings of the 16th conference on Computational linguistics - Volume 2*, COLING '96, pages 836–841, Stroudsburg, PA, USA. Association for Computational Linguistics.

N-gram and Gazetteer List Based Named Entity Recognition for Urdu: A Scarce Resourced Language

Faryal Jahangir[1], *Waqas Anwar*[1,2], *Usama Ijaz Bajwa*[1], *Xuan Wang*[2]
(1) COMSATS Institute of Information Technology, Abbottabad, University Road, Pakistan
(2)Harbin Institute of Technology Shenzhen Graduate School, P.R. China
faryaljahangir@ciit.net.pk, waqas@ciit.net.pk, usama@ciit.net.pk, xuanwang@insun.hit.edu.cn

ABSTRACT

Extraction of named entities (NEs) from the text is an important operation in many natural language processing applications like information extraction, question answering, machine translation etc. Since early 1990s the researchers have taken greater interest in this field and a lot of work has been done regarding Named Entity Recognition (NER) in different languages of the world. Unfortunately Urdu language which is a scarce resourced language has not been taken into account. In this paper we present a statistical Named Entity Recognition (NER) system for Urdu language using two basic n-gram models, namely unigram and bigram. We have also made use of gazetteer lists with both techniques as well as some smoothing techniques with bigram NER tagger. This NER system is capable to recognize 5 classes of NEs using a training data containing 2313 NEs and test data containing 104 NEs. The unigram NER Tagger using gazetteer lists achieves up to 65.21% precision, 88.63% recall and 75.14% f-measure. While the bigram NER Tagger using gazetteer lists and Backoff smoothing achieves up to 66.20% precision, 88.18% recall and 75.83 f-measure.

KEYWORDS : Named Entity Recognition, Unigram model, Bigram model, Gazetteer lists, smoothing techniques

1 Introduction

Named Entity Recognition (NER) is a task that locates and classifies the named entities ('atomic elements') in a text into predefined classes/categories like the names of persons, organizations, locations, expressions of times, quantities, etc. For example consider the following sentence:

"Microsoft launched its first retail version of Microsoft Windows on November 20, 1985"

An accurate NER system would extract two NEs from the above sentence: (i) "Microsoft" as an organization and (ii) "November 20, 1985" as a date. The ambiguous nature of named entities makes the NER task very difficult and challenging, and because of this problem most of the NER systems fail to attain human level performance. NER is a basic tool for all application areas of Natural Language Processing (NLP) such as Automatic Summarization, Machine Translation, Information Extraction, Information Retrieval, Question Answering, Text Mining, Genetics etc. Performance of all these applications depends on the performance of the NER system. These applications can perform well if the named entities are recognized and grouped accurately.

This work presents a statistical approach using n-gram for Urdu NER. The objective of this NER system is to recognize five classes of NEs – Person, Location, Organization, Date and Time. In this work unigram and bigram models are used for NER and NE tagged training data is used to train these models. When these trained models are tested using test data, the results do not show a high recall because of the inherent problems of Urdu language like lack of resources and rich morphology. To improve the results of the statistical models, gazetteer lists are used. Due to the fact that very less research work has been done in Urdu language in the field of NLP, therefore standard sized corpus like Brown is not available for Urdu. We also used some smoothing methods with bigram model to solve sparse data problem. The smoothing techniques chosen to solve data sparseness are: Add-one, Lidstone, Witten-Bell and back-off. Among all of these smoothing techniques only the back-off technique has improved the results of Urdu bigram NER system.

Rest of the paper is organized as follows. A brief survey of different techniques used for the NER task in different languages is presented in Section 2. A discussion on the challenges for Urdu NER is given in Section 3. The proposed n-gram based NER system is described in Section 4. In Section 5 and 6 we present the experimental results and related discussions. Finally Section 7 concludes the paper.

2 Related work

A number of different techniques have been used for the development of NER systems for different languages since 1991. A surfeit of algorithms has been developed for NER of English and other European languages and has achieved high recognition rates. Comparatively very few NER algorithms have been developed for South and South East Asian languages especially for Urdu language. The following section discusses earlier research carried out to develop NER systems for different languages.

2.1 Rule based approaches

Among the earlier research papers in the field of NER area, (Lisa and Jacobs, 1991) has presented a rule based NER system for identification and classification of different company names. The accuracy of system is over 95%. (Cucerzan and Yarowsky, 1999) developed a language independent NER system for Hindi language by using contextual and morphological evidences for five languages such as English, Greek, Romanian, Turkish and Hindi. The performance of Hindi NER system is very low and has f-measure of 41.70 with very low 27.84% recall and nearly 85% precision.

2.2 Statistical approaches

(Bortwick, 1999) presented a NER system based on Maximum Entropy (ME) for English language and has achieved F-measure of 84.22%. (Li and MacCallum, 2003) presented a Conditional Random Field (CRF) for the development of NER system for Hindi language. The system has 71.50% accuracy. The authors provided large array of lexical test and used feature induction for constructing the features automatically. (Nadeau et al., 2006) presented semi-supervised approach for the development of English NER system by classifying 100 named entities. The System has achieved F-measure value in the range 78-87%. (Saha et al., 2008) have used Maximum Entropy based NER system for Hindi language. The system has achieved F-value of 80.01% by using word selection and word clustering based feature reduction techniques. (Ekbal and Bandyopadhyay, 2008) have developed a statistical Conditional Random Field (CRF) model for the development of NER system for South and South East Asian languages, particularly for Bengali, Hindi, Telugu, Oriya and Urdu. The rules for identifying nested NEs for all the five languages and the gazetteer lists for Bengali and Hindi languages were used. The reported system achieved F-measure of 59.39% for Bengali,33.12 % for Hindi, 28.71% for Oriya, 4.749% for Telugu and 35.52 % for Urdu. (Goyal, 2008) developed CRF based NER system for Hindi language and evaluated it on test set1 and test set2 and achieved nested NEs F1-measure around 50.1% and maximal F1-measure around 49.2% for test set1 and nested NEs F1-measure around 43.70% and maximal F1 measure around 44.97 for test set2. (Gupta and Arora, 2009) presented a CRF based NER system for Hindi. The maximum F-measure achieved by the system is 66.7% for person, 69.5% for location and 58% for organization. (Raju et al. 2010) have developed ME based NER system for Telugu. The system has achieved an F-measure of 72.07% for person, 6.76%, 68.40% and 45.28% for organization, location and others respectively. (Ekbal and Saha et al., 2011) developed a multi-objective simulated annealing based classifier ensemble NER system for three scarce resourced languages like Hindi, Bengali and Telugu. The Recall, Precision and F-measure values are 93.95%, 95.15% and 94.55%, respectively for Bengali, 93.35%, 92.25% and 92.80%, respectively for Hindi and 84.02%, 96.56% and 89.85%, respectively for Telugu.

2.3 Hybrid approaches

(Bikel et al., 1997) developed IdentiFinder using HMM for English and Spanish languages to extract proper names and to make four categories including names, times, dates and numerical quantities. The system is reported to achieve F-measure of 90.44%. (Chaudhuri and Bhattachatya, 2008) developed NER system for Indian script Bangla. In which three-stage approach comprising of dictionary based, rules based and left-right co-occurrences statistics (n-gram) have been used for named entity. The system has achieved 85.50% recall, 94.24% precision and 89.51% f-measure. (Srikanth and Murthy, 2008) have used CRF based Noun Tagger for Telugu language using manually tagged data of 13,425 words for training and 6,223 words as test data. The system has F-value of Noun Tagger up to 92%. The rules based NER system has been developed for identifying names of person, place and organization. The overall F-measures of the system range between 80% to 97%. (Biswas et al., 2010) presented a hybrid system for Oriya NER based on ME, HMM and some handcrafted rules to recognize NEs. The system has an F-measure ranging between 75% to 90%. (Srivastava et al., 2011) presented hybrid approach for Hindi NER system. Rules were formulated over Conditional Random Field (CRF) model and Maximum Entropy (ME) model using features of POS and orthography for overcoming limitations of machine learning models for complex morphological languages like Hindi. The voting method has also been used to improve the performance of the NER system. Based on comparisons, CRF achieves better result than ME and rule based result.

2.4 Existing NE Systems for Urdu Language

Earlier research on NER for digital Urdu text has been carried out by (Becker and Riaz, 2002). Issues pertaining to Urdu language have been discussed and a corpus of 2200 Urdu documents has been developed. (Mukund et al., 2010) developed an information extraction system for Urdu language. The sub module of NER has been developed for information extraction system by using two models; namely ME and CRF based NER for Urdu. The result of ME has F-measures of 55.3% and the CRF based module for NER has F-measure value of 68.9%. (Riaz, 2010) has presented a rule based approach for Urdu NER system. Different rules have been formulated from 200 documents of Becker-Riaz corpus and have extracted 600 documents out of 2,262 documents for better evaluation during experimentation (Becker and Riaz, 2002). The system has f-measure of 91.1% with 90.7% recall and 91.5% precision. This rule based NER has achieved f-measures of 72.4% without any change in the rule set. The results have been later improved by developing new rules after analyzing the training set. The developed rule-based approach for Urdu NER shows encouraging results.

3 Challenges of Urdu NER

The large number of ambiguities of NE and the problems related to the Urdu language makes NER a challenging task. The construction of a robust Urdu NER is a complicated task because of the following limitations.

In English orthography capitalization of the initial letter is an indication that a word or sequence of words is a NE (Waqas et al., 2006). Urdu has no such indication which makes the detection of NEs more challenging. Thus, in Urdu language there is no difference between a NE and any other word from lexical point of view.

Some additional features can be added to the word to have more complex meaning. Agglutinative languages form sentences by adding a suffix to the root forms of the word. e.g. پا کستا ن(Pakistan is location) to پا کستا نی (Pakistani is person).

In Urdu Language SOV (Subject Object Verb) word order is used but usually the writers do not follow the same word order e.g. an English sentence "Ahmad closed the bag of books" can be written in Urdu"کتابوں کا بستہ احمد نے بند کیا" ("Kitabo ka basta Ahmad ne band kia") and "ا حمد نے کتابوں کا بستہ بند کیا"("Ahmad ne kitabo ka basta band kia"). The use of such different word orders makes the NE identification more challenging.

Some words are taken from other languages e.g. **(Palwasha)** پلو شہ is taken from Pushto language, **(Zeemal)** ز یمل is taken from Balochi language and **(Toyot)** ٹویوٹا is taken from English Language.

A nested name entity is composed of multiple words. This brings more challenges to accurately detect the beginning and the ending of a multi-word NE. To extract such NEs like محمد علی جناح*(person name)*and**(Name (Organization)** پشاور یونیورسٹی as single NE is difficult. The NER system commonly extracts such NEs as separate NEs such as پشاور (location name) and یونیورسٹی (organization name).

Some entities are made up by using conjunction word such as اور e.g. علی اوربلال سی این جی (organization name) is a conjunct NE which cannot be recognized as a single NE by the NER system.

A name entity can be used as a person name or organization name or as a word other than nouns e.g. نور is a name of person and also equivalent to the English word "light".

4 Proposed n-gram based Urdu NER tagger

4.1 Unigram Model

Unigram model is the simplest form of n-gram models based on probability estimation approach. The unigram NE tagger assigns the most probable NE tags to the NEs. It is trained on the training data to calculate the probabilities of NEs. The most probable NE tag for a NE is determined by calculating its probability with each NE tag. If the words in the corpus are given as $w_1, w_2, w_3, \ldots, w_n$ and their NE tags are represented as $t_1, t_2, t_3, \ldots, t_n$. Then the unigram model calculates the maximum probability $P(t_i \mid w_i)$ and selects the most probable tag for each NE.Units.

4.2 Bigram Model

Bigram model is another form of n-gram model also based on probability estimation approach. The bigram NE tagger assigns the most probable NE tags to the NEs by considering the last encountered word i-e the bigram models looks one word back for probability estimation. The bigram model determines the most probable NE tag for a NE by calculating word and its tag probability with the previous word. The bigram model calculates the maximum probability $P(w_i t_i \mid w_{i-1})$ and selects the most probable tag for each NE.

4.3 Use of Gazetteer Lists

Due to the issues of Urdu language discussed in section 4 the statistical techniques could not show better results especially in case of recall rate. Due to wide variations and the agglutinative nature of South Asian Languages, probabilistic graphical models result into a low less recall rates. The gazetteer lists have been used in this work to improve the recall. As compared to other languages especially European languages, Urdu language processing is not mature yet so the language processing resources like gazetteer lists are not available. These gazetteer lists were prepared from different sources including internet. Lists for the following name entities were prepared: person names, location names, organization names, date, time. The data collected from the internet is not enough so the NE tagged corpus was also used to populate the gazetteer lists.

4.4 Use of Smoothing Techniques

The N-gram language models use Maximum Likelihood Estimation (MLE) for probability estimation. If the data occurs regularly in the training corpus the Maximum Likelihood Estimation (MLE) works better. The MLE uses counts of n-grams in training data; if N-gram has a zero count then its probability will also be zero which is called data sparseness. Data sparseness is the main problem for N-gram models especially when the available corpus is small sized. Due to insufficient amount of training corpus, the data sparseness problem is faced. To solve sparse data problem we have used different smoothing techniques as in (Daniel and James, 2009). Some of them have improved the results of n-gram model but others failed to improve the results. (Chen and Goodman, 1996) carried out an extensive empirical comparison of the most widely used smoothing techniques. Following smoothing techniques are used in this work. Add-one, Lidstone, Witten-Bell and Back-off smoothing techniques.

5 Experimental results and properties of the corpus

5.1 Propertied of the Training and Test Corpus

A NE tagged corpus has been downloaded from the CRL. 179896 tokens that have 938 NEs of this corpus are used to train the system and other 4917 tokens having 220 NEs are used as test corpus. The training corpus has been divided into four different sets to train the n-gram models. First we have taken Set1 and trained the n-gram models with it and obtained the test results. Then we combine Set1 and Set2 to train the n-gram models and obtain the test results. After this we combine Set1, Set2 and Set3 to train the n-gram models and obtain the test results. At last we combine all the training data sets (Set1, Set2, Set3 and Set4) to train the n-gram models and obtain the test results. The testing data in all cases is same. The specification of these training data sets is given in the table 1 and the specification of testing corpus is given in table 2.

Training sets	Total no. of tokens	Total no. of NEs	Total no. of NNEs
Set1	7972	367	7605
Set2	8561	453	8108
Set3	11500	555	10945
Set4	17986	938	17048

TABLE 1- Specification of training corpus sets

Table 1 shows that set1 contains 7972 tokens; out of which there are 367 Named Entities and 7605 are not Named Entities.

Total no. of tokens	Total no. of NEs	Total no. of NNEs
4917	220	4697

TABLE 2- Specification of testing corpus

According to table 2 the testing corpus has 4917 tokens out of which 220 are NEs and the remaining 4697 tokens are not NEs. The tag set used is described in table 3

Tag	Name	Description
</PERSON>	Person	عامر محمود، صدام Sadaam ,Mehmood ,Amir
</LOCATION>	Location	پاکستان ، اسلام آباد، نئی دہلی Pakistan, Islamabad, New Dehli
</ORGANIZATION>	Organization	مجلس عمل، لاہور ہائی کورٹ،
</DATE>	Date	پیر، جنوری، گیارہ ستمبر دو ہزار ایک
</TIME>	Time	نو بجے، شب، صبح

TABLE 3- NE tag set

5.2 Evaluation Metrics

Before presenting the experimental results the evaluation parameters used for result's evaluation are discussed in this section. Massage Understanding Conference (MUC) and Multilingual Entity (MET) used the terms Precision (P) and Recall (R) from information retrieval research community which are now being used as evaluation metrics for performance of NER systems. Our NER system is evaluated in terms of precision, recall and f-measure.

5.3 Results of Unigram NER Tagger

The overall results of unigram NER Tagger with above specified training and testing data are given in Table4

No. of Tokens/No. of NEs	Precision	Recall	F-measure
7972/367	89.33	30.45	45.85
16533/820	89.53	35	50.33

28033/1375	88.46	41.81	56.79
46019/2313	85.71	49.09	59.09

TABLE 4- Results using simple unigram NER Tagger

The overall results by using unigram NER Tagger along with gazetteer lists are given in table 5.

No. of Tokens/No. of NEs	Precision	Recall	F-measure
7972/367	65.52	87.27	74.85
16533/820	65.87	88.63	75.58
28033/1375	65.99	89.09	75.82
46019/2313	65.21	88.63	75.14

TABLE 5-Results using unigram NER Tagger along with gazetteer lists

The results we obtained for different types of NEs using unigram NER Tagger along with gazetteer lists are given in table 6.

Types of NEs	Precision	Recall	F-measure
Location	85.04	94.79	89.65
Person	48.734	90.58	63.37
Organization	80	44.44	57.14
Time	66.66	100	80.00
Date	87.5	63.63	73.68

TABLE 6 -Results using unigram NER Tagger along with gazetteer lists for different types of NEs

5.4 Results of Bigram NER Tagger

The overall results of the simple bigram NER Tagger are given in Table 7

No. of Tokens/No. of NEs	Precision	Recall	F-Measure
7972/367	90.91	9.09	16.5
16533/820	88.89	10.91	19.44
28033/1375	92.31	16.37	27.78
46019/2313	88	20	32.59

TABLE 7- Overall results using bigram NER Tagger

The overall results obtained after applying gazetteer lists to the tagged data returned by bigram NER tagger are given in Table 8.

No. of Tokens/No. of NEs	Precision	Recall	F-Measure
7972/367	65.26	84.54	73.66
16533/820	65.38	85	73.91
28033/1375	65.38	85	73.91
46019/2313	64.58	84.54	73.23

TABLE 8- Results using bigram NER Tagger along with gazetteer lists

The overall results by using bigram NER Tagger along with gazetteer lists and Backoff Smoothing are given in table 9.

No. of Tokens/No. of NEs	Precision	Recall	F-Measure
7972/367	65.39	85.90	74.26
16533/820	65.8	87.72	75.24
28033/1375	66.10	88.63	75.72
46019/2313	66.20	88.18	75.83

Table 9 Overall results using bigram NER Tagger along with gazetteer lists and Backoff Smoothing

The results we obtained for different types of NEs using bigram NER Tagger along with gazetteer lists and Backoff Smoothing are given in table 10.

Types of NEs	Precision	Recall	F-measure
Location	84.07	98.95	90.90
Person	49.04	90.58	63.63
Organization	93.33	38.88	54.90
Time	100	50	66.66
Date	87.67	63.63	73.75

TABLE 10-Results using bigram NER Tagger along with gazetteer lists and Backoff smoothing for different types of NEs

6 Discussion

From Table 4 and 7 we can see that simple unigram and bigram models produce a high precision but the recall is very low in both cases because of small sized training data. To improve our recall we used gazetteer lists along with unigram and bigram Taggers. By using the gazetteer list the recall of the taggers improved but at the cost of precision. Here the precision decreases because our tagger looks the gazetteers one by one in a sequence and tags a word with respect to the type of the list in which it finds the words first without any confirmation whether it's the right tag for that word or not. Resultantly it tags many words incorrectly which decreases the recall. As compared to unigram Tagger, bigram Tagger show very low recall, because the bigram NER Tagger uses word bigram for probability calculation so it needs more training data as compared to unigram NER Tagger. Since we have a small sized training corpus, so the bigram NER Tagger finds only some of the NE bigrams in training corpus and tags them with appropriate tags and misses a large number of NEs due to data sparseness. To solve this sparse data problem some smoothing techniques were tested with bigram model and among all the techniques tested, only back off smoothing improved the results. From the results, it is evident that as the size of training data increased the results of the taggers got better. But in case of training Set4, the results especially recall decreased, because the NEs present in training Set4 create more ambiguity, as they belong to more than one type of NE classes depending on the context in which they are used.

Conclusion

In this research work we presented a statistical NER tagger for Urdu language. There are various issues related to Urdu language processing, including lack of standard Urdu corpus and incompatibility issues of NLP tools for Urdu language which has been discussed earlier. In this work NER for Urdu text has been implemented using unigram and bigram statistical models. Significant results have been produced even with a small sized training data. Low recall and sparse data problems occur due to the inherent issues of Urdu language like unavailability of sufficient resources. To solve sparse data problem we tested different smoothing techniques and the backoff smoothing technique proved beneficial. We also used gazetteer lists to improve the results of n-gram statistical models. The unigram tagger trained with training data and combined with gazetteers produced up to 65.217% precision, 88.636% recall and 75.144% f-measure. A bigram NER tagger is trained with training data, combined with gazetteers and Backoff smoothing produced up to 66.205% precision, 88.181% recall and 75.834% f-measure.

References

D. Becker, K. Riaz. (2002). A study in urdu corpus construction. Proceedings *of the 3rd Workshop on Asian Language Resources and International Standardization*, pages 1–5.

DM. Bikel, S. Miller, R. Schwartz, , R. Weischedel. (1997). Nymble: a high-performance learning name-finder. *In Proceedings of the fifth Conference on Applied Natural Language Processing*, pages 194-201.

S. Biswas, S. Mishra, S. Acharya, S. Mohanty. (2010). A hybrid oriya named entity recognition system: harnessing the power of rule Biswas". *International Journal of Artificial Intelligence and Expert Systems*. 1(1): 1-6.

A. Borthwick. (1999). A maximum entropy approach to named entity recognition. New York University.

BB. Chaudhuri, S. Bhattacharya. (2008). An experiment on automatic detection of named entities in Bangla. *In Proceedings of the IJCNLP Workshop on NER for South and South East Asian Languages*, pages 75-81.

SF. Chen, J. Goodman. (1996). An empirical study of smoothing techniques for language modeling. *Proceedings of the 34th annual meeting on Association for Computational Linguistics*, pages 310-318.

S. Cucerzan, D. Yarowsky. (1999). Language independent named entity recognition combining morphological and contextual evidence. *Proceedings of the Joint SIGDAT conference on EMNLP and VLC,* pages 90-99.

J. Daniel, HM. James. (2009). *Speech and language processing: an introduction to natural language processing, computational linguistics and speech recognition* (2nd.). Prentice Hall.

Ekbal A, Bandyopadhyay S. (2008). Bengali named entity recognition using conditional random field. *In Proceedings of the IJCNLP Workshop on NER for South and South East Asian Languages,* pages 589-594.

A. Ekbal, S. Saha. (2011). A multiobjective simulated annealing approach for classifier ensemble: Named entity recognition in Indian languages as case studies. Expert *Systems with Applications*. 38(12): 14760-14772.

Goyal. (2008). Named entity recognition for SouthAsian languages. *Proceedings of the IJCNLP Workshop on NER for South and South East Asian Languages*, pages 89-96.

Gupta PK, Arora S. (2009). An approach for named entity recognition system for Hindi: an experimental study. *In Proceedings of the ASCNT,* pages 103 –108.

Li W, McCallum A. (2003). Rapid development of Hindi named entity recognition using conditional random fields and feature induction. *In ACM Transactions on Asian Language Information Processing*. 2(3): 290-294.

Lisa FR, Jacobs SP. (1991). Creating segmented databases from free text for text retrieval. *Proceedings of the 14th annual international ACM SIGIR conference on Research and development in information retrieval,* pages 337--346.

Mukund S, Srihari R, Peterson E. (2010). An Information-extraction system for Urdu—a resource-poor language. *In ACM Transactions on Asian Language Information Processing*. 9(4):15.

Nadeau D, Turney P, Matwin S (2006). Unsupervised named-entity recognition: generating gazetteers and resolving ambiguity. *Canadian Conference on Artificial Intelligence*, pages 266-277.

Raju SB, Raju DSV, Kumar, K (2010). Named entity recognition for Telegu using maximum entropy model. *Journal of Theoretical and Applied Information Technology*. 13(2): 125-130

Riaz K. (2010). Rule-based named entity recognition in Urdu. *In Proceedings of the Named Entities Workshop*. pages 126-135.

Saha SK, Sudeshna S, Mitra P. (2008). A hybrid feature set based maximum entropy Hindi named entity recognition. *Proceedings of the Third International Joint Conference on Natural Language Processing*, Pages 343-349

Srikanth P, Murthy KN. (2008). Named entity recognition for Telugu. *Proceedings of the IJCNLP Workshop on NER for South and South East Asian Languages*, pages 41-50.

Srivastava S, Sanglikar M, Kothari D. (2011). Named entity recognition system for Hindi language: a hybrid approach. *International Journal of Computational Linguistics*. 2(1): 10-23.

Waqas A, Xuan W, Xiao-long W. (2006). A Survey of Automatic Urdu language processing. *International Conference on Machine Learning and Cybernetics*, pages 4489-4494.

Developing a POS tagger for Magahi: A Comparative Study

Ritesh KUMAR[1] *Bornini LAHIRI*[1] *Deepak ALOK*[1]
(1) CENTRE FOR LINGUISTICS, Jawharlal Nehru University, India
ritesh78_llh@jnu.ac.in, lahiri.bornini@gmail.com,
deepak06alok@gmail.com

ABSTRACT

In this paper, we present a comparative study of the four state-of-the-art sequential taggers applied on Magahi data for part-of-speech (POS) annotation . Magahi is one of the smaller Indo-Aryan languages spoken in Eastern state of Bihar in India. It is an extremely resource-poor language and it is the first attempt to develop some kind of Natural Language Processing (NLP) resource for the language.

The four taggers that we test are – Support Vector Machines (SVM) based SVMTool, Hidden Markov Model (HMM) based TnT tagger, Maximum Entropy based MxPost tagger and Memory based MBT tagger. All these taggers are trained on a miniscule dataset of around 50,000 words using 33 tags from the BIS-tagset for Indian languages and tested on around 13,000 words. The performance of all these taggers are tested against a frequency-based baseline tagger. While all these taggers perform worse than on the English data, the best performance is given by the Maximum Entropy tagger after tuning of certain parameters. The paper discusses the result of the taggers and the ways in which the performance of the taggers could be improved for Magahi.

KEYWORDS : POS TAGGERS, MAGAHI TAGGER, SVM, TNT TAGGER, MXPOST TAGGER, MBT TAGGER

1 Introduction

Historically, Magahi has been classified in different ways by different scholars. While Grierson (1903) puts Magahi under the Eastern group of Outer sub-branch of Indo-Aryan languages, others like Turner have clubbed the 'Bihari' languages with Eastern and Western Hindi (Masica 1991). A classification given by Chatterji (1926) where Magahi is kept together with other languages of Eastern group which is separate from the Western Hindi. Jeffers (1976) gives a classification which is very similar to that of Grierson.

In the present time, Magahi is spoken mainly in Eastern states of India including Bihar and Jharkhand, along with some parts of West Bengal and Orissa. There are three main varieties of Magahi spoken today (Verma, 1991).

- Central Magahi of Patna, Gaya, Hazaribagh (in Bihar)
- South-Eastern Magahi of Ranchi (in Jharkhand) and some parts of Orissa
- Eastern Magahi of Begusarai and Munger (in Bihar)

Some other scholars like Verma (2003) and Grierson (1903) have also classified South-Eastern and Eastern varieties together.

1.1 Magahi: Socio-Political Situation

Socially Magahi is considered a dialect of Hindi even though historically as well as linguistically Magahi distinct enough from Hindi to be called a distinct language. This social attitude towards Magahi where it is considered a dialect (and inferior/distorted form) of Hindi has emanated largely from the political representation of the language as a dialect (or, Mother Tongue in the Census) of Hindi as well as the close lexical affinity of the two languages (Kumar, et.al., 2011). As a result of this socio-political attitude, Magahi has remained a largely ignored language outside linguistic studies despite the presence of quite a large population (counting up to 13.978,565 according to Census of India, 2001) of Magahi speakers.

1.2 Linguistic Features of Magahi

There has been very few linguistic studies on Magahi. However a basic (although not completely accurate) description of Magahi is given by Verma (2003). A basic description of the linguistic features is given here.

An initial analysis of the Magahi sound system shows that it has 35 phonemic sounds – 27 consonants and 8 vowels. Some of the major phonlogical features which distinguish Magahi from Hindi include absence of word-initial consonant cluster, absence of word-initial glides and absence of word-medial and word-final dental laterals.

Morphologically it is a nominative-accusative, inflected language with almost free word order of constituents within phrases and sentences. Both nouns and adjectives have two basic forms. While one form is the basic form (as in *g^hora* 'horse', *sona* 'gold', *ʊɟər* 'white', etc), the other one is the derived form (as in *g^hor-ba, son-ma, ʊɟər-ka*). The affixes used in the derived forms are the affixal particles which are used for different linguistic function like specificity, definiteness etc (Alok, 2010, 2012).

Unlike Hindi (which is a Noun Class language with two classes, also equated with Masculine and Feminine gender in the language), Magahi is a classifier language. It has three mensural classifiers – *go/t^{h}o, məni, sun* (Alok, 2012). These classifiers encode the information about how the referent is measured and are different from the other generally found classifiers which characterise noun in terms of certain inherent properties (Aikhenvald, 2000, 2006). Among these while *go/t^{h}o* measures nouns in terms of length or discrete quantity, *məni* and *sun* are used for measuring nouns in terms of amount (and so are used with the mass nouns) (Alok, 2012). It is to be noted that broadly these are numeral classifiers since they are always attached with the numeral and quantifiers in a noun phrase and never with the noun itself. The presence of classifiers could prove to be a very strong indicator for the Part-of-speech annotation of quantifiers and Noun in Magahi.

Syntactically, Magahi nouns do not have number and gender agreement with verbs. There are only a few nouns in Magahi which could be inflected for number. Moreover adjectives also agree with such nouns in terms of number as well as sex (it should be noted here that sex here refers to the natural sex of the noun in case of animates and not the Noun class as it is used for Hindi since such agreements could occur only with the animates for which males and females are distinctly recognised in the language). Verbs also agree with subjects in person and honorificity. It is to be noted that verbs could also agree with object as well as addressee honorificity of the object or the addressee are honorific.

1.3 Part-of-speech Annotation and Magahi

Part-of-speech annotation is generally considered the most basic step for developing any kind of NLP application. In the recent times several statistical and machine-learning based approaches have been applied to the task of POS annotation. Some of the major and most successful taggers include - Hidden Markov Models (Brants, 2000), Maximum Entropy taggers (Ratnaparkhi, 1996), Transformation–based learning (Brill, 1994, 1995), Memory–based learning (Daelemans, et. al., 2003), Support Vector Machines (Cortes & Vapnik, 2000) besides several others.

All these taggers are trained and evaluated on the WSJ corpus in English. On this corpus all of these have a very comparable accuracy with each giving only slightly different accuracy from the others. In this paper, we have applied Magahi data to four of these POS tagers, viz, HMM tagger, MaxEnt Tagger, Memory-based Tagger and SVM, for the purpose of developing a POS tagger for Magahi. The idea is to test which of these give the best performance on the given dataset with their default settings. The performance is compared against a Maximum-frequency baseline tagger.

2 Experimental Setup

2.1 Dataset

We have used around 50,000 manually POS-tagged data for training each of the tagger and they are tested on around 11,000 words. The corpus consists of data taken from a collection of Magahi folktales. Since Magahi is largely a spoken language and there is very scant availability of written material, the collection of folktales was the most readily available as well as standardised written data available.

2.2 Tagset

For the annotation of Magahi data, we have used a modified version of BIS standard tagset for Indian Languages. The complete tagset, which consists of 33 tags, is given in Table 1 (the corpus tagged with this tagset is same as described in Kumar, et al. (2011) but the tagset is slightly modified).

Sl. No	**Category**		**Label**	**Annotation Convention**	Examples (in IPA)
	Top level	Subtype (level 1)			
1	**Noun**		**N**	**N**	c^hɔːɽɑ (boy)
1.1		Common	NN	N__NN	cəcəriː (a small bridge-like st.) ləŋgte (naked)
1.2		Proper	NNP	N__NNP	p^huləva
1.3		Nloc	NST	N__NST	əgaɽiː, pic^{h}aɽiː
2	**Pronoun**		**PR**	**PR**	
2.1		Personal	PRP	PR__PRP	həm, həməniː
2.2		Reflexive	PRF	PR__PRF	əpəne
2.3		Relative	PRL	PR__PRL	ɟe, ɟekər
2.4		Reciprocal	PRC	PR__PRC	əpəne
2.5		Wh-word	PRQ	PR__PRQ	kɑ, ke
2.6		Indefinite	PRI	PR__PRI	koi, kekrɑ

3	**Demonstrative**		**DM**	**DM**	
3.1		Deictic	DMD	DM__DMD	ĩhã, ʊ̃hã
3.2		Relative	DMR	DM__DMR	ɟe, ɟəun
3.3		Wh-word	DMQ	DM__DMQ	kekrɑ, kəun
3.4		Indefinite	DMI	DM__DMI	i, ʊ
4	**Verb**		**V**	**V**	ləuknɑ (to see)
4.1		Main	VM	V__VM	p^{h}ĩcnɑ (to wash clothes) əɟ^{h}urɑnɑ (to get entangled)
4.2		Auxiliary	VAUX	V__VAUX	həi, həliː, hət̪^{h}iː
5	**Adjective**		**JJ**	**JJ**	cəkəit^h (short and well-built) bət̪p^{h}əros (uselessly talkative)
6	**Adverb**		**RB**	**RB**	cəb^{h}ɑk (with splash) cəb^{h}ər-cəb^{h}r (a manner of eating)
7	**Postposition**		**PSP**	**PSP**	ke, me, pər, ɟore
8	**Conjunction**		**CC**	**CC**	
8.1		Co-ordinator	CCD	CC__CCD	ɑʊ, bɑkiː, bəluk
8.2		Subordinator	CCS	CC__CCS	kɑheki, t̪ə, ki
9	**Particles**		**RP**	**RP**	
9.1		Default	RPD	RP__RPD	t̪ə, b^{h}iː

9.2		Classifier	CL	RP__CL	go, tʰo
9.3		Interjection	INJ	RP__INJ	əre, he, cʰi:, bɑpre
9.4		Intensifier	INTF	RP__INTF	təhtəh, tuhtuh, bʰək-bʰək
9.5		Negation	NEG	RP__NEG	nə, mət̪, binɑ
10	**Quantifiers**		**QT**	**QT**	ek, pəhilɑ, kucʰ
10.1		General	QTF	QT__QTF	təni:sun, dʰerməni:
10.2		Cardinals	QTC	QT__QTC	ek, du, igɑrəh
10.3		Ordinals	QTO	QT__QTO	pəhilɑ, dʊsrɑ
11	**Residuals**		**RD**	**RD**	
11.1		Foreign word	RDF	RD__RDF	A word in foreign script.
11.2		Symbol	SYM	RD__SYM	For symbols such as $, & etc
11.3		Punctuation	PUNC	RD__PUNC	Only for punctuations
11.4		Unknown	UNK	RD__UNK	
11.5		Echowords	ECH	RD__ECH	(pɑni:-) uni: (kʰɑnɑ-) unɑ

TABLE 1: Magahi Tagset

2.3 Tagger Tools

We have used the following tools to train different taggers on Magahi data -

- MxPost for Maximum-entropy tagger (Ratnaparkhi, 1996). It uses the contextual features like preceeding words and tags as well as morphological feature of the words like the suffixes and prefixes for tagging any given word.
- MBT for Memory-based tagger (Daelemans, et. al., 2003). It creates two separate taggers after the training. One is used exclusively for known words and it uses the

contextual features and the other is used exclusively for unknown words which also uses lexical information alongwith the contextual features. These features are customisable as per the need of the users

- TnT for HMM-based tagger (Brants, 1994). As the name of the tagger itself suggest (Trigrams 'n' Tags), it uses trigram and the tags of the preceding words as features for training
- SVMTool for SVM-based tagger (Gimenez and Marquez, 2004). This tool provides an interface for using SVM-Light (Joachims, 1999). The features that could be used with this tool is similar to the other tools, viz., morphological features of the word and that of the context as well as the tags of the preceding words.

In general we have used these tools with the default/recommended settings for carrying out the experiments. Each of these tools were trained on exactly the same corpus consisting of around 50,000 tokens.

3 Results and Analysis

The results obtained from the four tools are summarised in Table 2 below

	Known Words (86 %)	**Unknown Words (14%)**	**Overall**
TnT	89.75%	67.57%	86.09%
MBT	89.15%	72.97%	86.22%
MxPost	NA	NA	**89.61%**
SVMTool	81.89%	18.11%	**41.46%**
Baseline	NA	NA	71.18%

TABLE 2: Comparison of the taggers

As mentioned above each tagger was also tested on exactly the same dataset which consisted of around 13,000 tokens. Out of these 13,000 tokens around 86% were known tokens (i.e. they were present in the training set also) while 14% were unknown token (they were encountered by the tagger for the first time in the test set itself). As it is shown in the table, MxPost gives the best overall performance; however since the evaluation results are not calculated separately for known and unknown words the break-up is not known. MBT and TnT gives comparable overall results but MBT is significantly more accurate with unknown words. The most dismal performance is given by SVMTool which could be explained only by an extremely small dataset and presence of a large number of classes which needs to be classified.

An error analysis of the data shows that the major source of error in the annotation is the serial verb constructions in all the three taggers. While MxPost performs slightly better, in general, detection of second verb (if it is a compound verb) or the noun of the second verb complex (if it is a conjunct verb) proved to be very problematic. Another source of error was a complete absence of examples of certain closed-class categories in the training set viz., interjections. Besides these two, as expected, lexical ambiguity was also one of the minor sources of annotation error.

Conclusion and Way Ahead

In this paper we have presented a comparison of the four state-of-the-art POS taggers with respect to their performance on the Magahi data. The best overall accuracy as well as accuracy on the known and unknown words individually is given by the maximum-entropy based MxPost tagger. However the accuracy (just below 90%) is much below the general expected accuracy of POS taggers. As the error analysis shows all the taggers perform poorly on very similar kinds of words. So combining different taggers could not solve the problem. The two steps which could be taken to increase the accuracy of the tagger include

- A list of closed-class words will be prepared which would be able to handle the cases where the absence of the word in training set has led to the error by the tagger.
- Some explicit disambiguation rules will also be used in certain cases where sufficiently large number of examples is not present in the training corpus so as to discriminate in between the contexts of occurrence of a particular tag of the word.

A third possible step could be to increase the training set size (which is in any case pretty small by the general standards). However this is very resource-intensive because of the lack of easily available data in the language. Moreover as per our current analysis a hybrid system like this is expected to give a performance at par with most of the other state-of-the-art POS taggers for Indian languages.

Acknowledgments

We would like to thank our supervisors for their constant support and guidance.

References

Alok, D. (2010). Magahi Noun Particles. Paper presented in *4th International Students' Conference of Linguistics in India (SCONLI-4)*, Mumbai, India, February 20-22, 2010.

Alok, D. (2012). *A language without Articles: The Case of Magahi*. Unpublished M.Phil. Dissertation, Jawaharlal Nehru University, New Delhi

Brants , T.. (2000). TnT — A Statistical Part-of-Speech Tagger. In *Proceedings of the 6th Applied NLP Conference(ANLP-2000)*, pages 224–231.

Brill, E. (1994). Some Advances in Transformation-Based Part of Speech Tagging. *Proceedings of AAAI*, Vol. 1, pages 722–727.

Brill, E. (1995). Transformation-Based Error-Driven Learning and Natural Language Processing: A Case Study in Part-of-Speech Tagging. *Computational Linguistics*, 21(4): 543–565.

Cortes , C. and Vapnik, V. (1995). Support Vector Networks. *Machine Learning*, 20: 273–297.

Daelemans, W., Zavrel, J., van den Bosch, A., van der Sloot, K. (2003). MBT: Memory Based Tagger, version 2.0, *Reference Guide. ILK Research Group Technical Report Series 03-13*, Tilburg.

Jesus Gimenez and Lluis Marquez. (2004). SVMTool: A general POS tagger generator based on support vector machines. In *4th International Conference on Language Resources and Evaluation*, pages 168–176, Lisbon, Portugal.

Joachims, T. (1999). Making Large-scale SVM Learning Practical. In Schölkopf, B., Burges, C., Smola, A., eds.: *Advances in Kernel Methods – Support Vector Learning*, pages 41–56. MIT Press, Boston, MA, USA .

Kumar, R., Lahiri, B. and Alok, D. (2011). Challenges in Developing LRs for Non-Scheduled Languages: A Case of Magahi. In *Proceedings of the 5th Language and Technology Conference Human Language Technologies as a Challenge for Computer Science and Linguistics (LTC '11)*, Adam Mickiewicz University, pages 60-64.

Ratnaparkhi, A. (1996). A maximum entropy model for part-of-speech tagging. In *Proceedings of the Conference on Empirical Methods in Natural Language Processing*, University of Pennsylvania, pages 133–142.

Enhancing Lemmatization for Mongolian and its Application to Statistical Machine Translation

Odbayar Chimeddorj Atsushi Fujii
Graduate School of Information Science and Engineering, Tokyo Institute of Technology
2-12-1 Ookayama, 152-8552, Japan
chimeddorj.o.aa AT m.titech.ac.jp

ABSTRACT

Lemmatization is crucial in natural language processing and information retrieval especially for highly inflected languages, such as Finnish and Mongolian. The state-of-the-art method of lemmatization for Mongolian does not need a noun dictionary and is scalable, but errors of this method are mainly caused by problems related to part of speech (POS) information. To resolve this problem, we integrate POS tagging and lemmatization for Mongolian. We evaluate the effectiveness of our method and its contribution to statistical machine translation.

KEYWORDS : Morphological segmentation, Lemmatization, Mongolian language, Statistical Machine Translation.

1 Introduction

In Mongolian, two different alphabets are used, Cyrillic and Mongolian. While the Cyrillic alphabet is mainly used in Mongolia, the Mongolian alphabet is mainly used in the Inner Mongolian Autonomous Region of China. Depending on the alphabet used, the writing system is also different in Mongolian. In this paper, we focus only on the Mongolian language that uses the Cyrillic alphabet, which will be termed "Mongolian" hereafter.

In Mongolian, which is an agglutinative language, each sentence is segmented on a phrase-by-phrase basis. A phrase consists of a content word, such as a noun or a verb, and one or more suffixes, such as postpositional participles. A content word can potentially be inflected when concatenated with suffixes.

Identifying the original forms of content words is crucial for natural language processing and information retrieval. In information retrieval, normalizing index terms can involve either lemmatization or stemming. Lemmatization identifies the original form of an inflected word, whereas stemming identifies a stem, which is not necessarily a word. Lemmatization is especially crucial for highly inflected languages, such as Finish and Mongolian. For example, one of the longest phrases in Mongolian "хамтралжуулагдсанаараа" consists of a stem (хам-), four derivational (-т -р -(а)л -ж) and five inflectional (-уул - (а)гд -сан -аар -аа) suffixes. This phrase is translated into 11 words in English as in the following example sentence.

Mongolian:	Тосгоныхон *хамтралжуулагдсанаараа* илүү сайн амьдрах болов.
English:	Village people, in that they were caused to be organized into collective farms, improved their lives.

In this paper, we enhance an existing lemmatization method for Mongolian by using parts of speech annotation and apply our method to statistical machine translation for English to Mongolian.

2 Related work

Ehara et al. (2007) proposed a morphological analysis method for Mongolian-to-Japanese transfer-based machine translation. Ehara et al. manually produced Mongolian morphological inflectional rules, a suffix dictionary, and a lexicon for a morphological analyzer for Japanese. Their method uses these resources and lemmatizes an input phrase to generate its Japanese translation phrase by transferring the morphological structure.

Purev et al. (2005) proposed a method for morphological analysis targeting Mongolian using PC-KIMMO (Antworth, 1990). PC-KIMMO is based on a finite-state two-level morphological description approach (Koskenniemi, 1983). Purev et al. produced 36 two-level morphological rules for Mongolian, and used a lexicon consisting of 29,266 words (6,199 nouns, 18,551 verbs, and 4,516 adjectives) and 223 affixes. The accuracy of Purev et al's method for two novels was 60.5%. Errors were mainly due to out-of-dictionary words and contradictions between manually-written rules.

Sanduijav et al. (2005) proposed a lemmatization method for Mongolian verbs and nouns. This method uses a dictionary that was automatically produced by generating every possible combination of words and suffixes with manually-written morphological rules. Like Purev et al., this method also does not correctly lemmatize out-of-dictionary words.

Khaltar and Fujii (2009) proposed a state-of-the-art lemmatization method for Mongolian, which uses a suffix dictionary and a number of rules for suffix segmentation and vowel insertion. Unlike the above methods, this method does not need a noun dictionary and is therefore scalable. In addition, Khaltar and Fujii showed that their method experimentally outperformed Sanduijav et al. (2005). Therefore, we enhance Khaltar and Fujii's method with parts of speech information, and explain the method in details in following.

Given a phrase consisting of a content word and one or more suffixes, Khaltar and Fujii's method removes the suffixes and extracts the content word. In addition, the rules are used to identify the original form of the extracted content word. However, because details of the lemmatization process can vary depending on the part of speech (POS) for the target content word, a verb dictionary is used to determine whether the target content word is a verb or not. Because new verbs are created less frequently than nouns, they use a verb dictionary, but not a noun dictionary. Thus, this method is robust against out-of-dictionary words, compared with other existing methods.

However, Khaltar and Fujii's method is associated with three problems. First, their method often misrecognizes an out-of-dictionary verb as a noun and consequently lemmatizes the target phrase incorrectly. Second, their method incorrectly lemmatizes a content word that is associated with more than one POS. For example, a phrase "орон" is either a verb phrase consisting of "ор" (to enter) and "он" (serial verb suffix) or a noun phrase consisting of only a noun "орон" (country), as shown in examples (1) and (2), respectively. We also show an English translation below each sentence.

(1) дотогш ор+он алга болов
Verb+Suffix
(someone) went inside and disappeared

(2) олон орон цөмийн эрчим хүч хэрэглэдэг
Noun
many countries use nuclear energy

For another example, the word "хамгийн" in Mongolian means "most" in English, and its syntactic function is superlative for adjectives and adverbs. Because its lexical structure is same as "хамаг" (whole or all) + "-ийн" (genitive case), "хамгийн" can be misrecognized as a noun concatenated with an inflectional suffix. Third problem is related to phrases that have the same surface form and POS but different meaning and morphological structure. For example, the word "уусан" can be two different inflected verbs depending on the context, as shown below.

(3) уух + сан → уусан
to drink + past tense → drank
Би өчигдөр анх удаа япон ногоон цай уусан
Yesterday, I drank Japanese green tea for the first time.

(4) уусах + н → уусан
to fade/melt + serial verb suffix → faded and [another verb]
Мөс усанд уусан алга болов
Ice melted into water and disappeared.

In the above examples, knowing only the POS of "уусан" is insufficient to segment it correctly even consulting to the verb dictionary because both usages in (3) and (4) are verbs. Therefore, it is necessary to know its inflection from the sentence content.

3 Our method for lemmatization

To resolve the three problems associated with Khaltar and Fujii (2009) described in Section 2, we combine their method and POS tagging. For the first problem, we can use POS information to distinguish nouns and verbs in target phrases. For the second problem, we can identify the POS for an ambiguous word depending on the context and use the corresponding lemmatization process. For the third problem, the POS annotation used in our method includes inflectional structure for verbs and nouns. For example, a POS annotation for a noun phrase is distinguished whether it is inflected or not. If inflected, the POS annotation also carries inflection type such as plural, genitive, and possessive.

In practice, we perform POS tagging for an input sentence and then use Khaltar and Fujii's method to perform lemmatization on a phrase-by-phrase basis. Training the POS tagging needs only POS annotated corpus, instead it does not need lemmatization. Our method consists of three components: POS annotation of input sentence, extracting target phrases with their POS information and lemmatizing target phrase by Khaltar and Fujii's method. The procedure of our lemmatization method is shown in following with a step-by-step example.

Step 1. олон орон цөмийн эрчим хүч хэрэглэдэг
Many countries use nuclear energy

Step 2. олон орон цөмийн эрчим хүч хэрэглэдэг
JJ N NG N N VP

Step 3. олон орон цөмийн эрчим хүч хэрэглэдэг
nuclear+genitive to use+present
N NG N N VP

Step 4. олон орон цөм+ийн эрчим хүч хэрэглэ+дэг
N+genitive V+present

In the above example, a sentence in Mongolian is segmented through three steps. Step 1 is POS tagging on an input sentence. Step 2 is extracting target phrases with their POS information. In Step 3, the target phrases are lemmatized by Khaltar and Fujii's method by consulting with POS information. As shown in the example, two target phrases are identified according to POS annotation: цөмийн and хэрэглэдэг ("nuclear" and "to use" in English, respectively). The example also shows examples of (1) and (2) mentioned in Section 2. The phrase орон ("countries" in English) is incorrectly lemmatized as a verb instead of noun in Khaltar and Fujii's method.

4 Experiments

4.1 Overview

We conducted two separate experiments to evaluate our lemmatization method for Mongolian. In Section 4.2, our method is evaluated on lemmatizing verb and noun phrases, and the result is compared to the Khaltar and Fujii's method. In Section 4.3, we evaluate the effectiveness of Khaltar and Fujii's and our methods in statistical machine translation (SMT).

For POS tagging purpose, we used a statistical POS tagger "TnT" (Thorsten, 2000) and a 5 M word Mongolian corpus, in which each word is manually annotated with its POS tag and inflectional structure (Jaimai and Chimeddorj, 2008), for training purposes. This corpus consists of common domains such as laws, novels and news.

4.2 Evaluating lemmatization accuracy

In the evaluation of lemmatization, we used the same test data as in Khaltar and Fujii (2009), which consists of 183 newspaper articles (hereafter "News") and 1,467 technical abstracts (hereafter "Tech") for Mongolian. Furthermore, we targeted on the noun and verb phrases of the test data due to the most inflectional POS in Mongolian and the NLP and IR application. The amount of the targeted phrases is shown in Table 1.

Test data	Noun phrase		Verb phrase	
	In types	In tokens	In types	In tokens
News	5,201	14,538	5,086	11,723
Tech	15,982	73,625	4,797	37,477
Total	21,899	86,554	9,880	49,200

TABLE 1 – Target phrase types and tokens for the experiment.

As shown in Table 1, we targeted on 31,779 types of phrases of which 21,899 are noun phrases and 9,880 are verb phrases, respectively.

First, the test data was tagged with the TnT. We found that the accuracy for POS tagging was 93.8%. Second, the phrases shown in Table 4 were extracted from News and Tech with their POS tags, and each of them was given to the lemmatization method with its POS information. Finally, the result of the lemmatization was compared with human assessed correct answers. The total accuracy of Khaltar and Fujii's method was 73.4% while that of our method was 86.6%, as shown in Table 2. Furthermore, the accuracy of lemmatization for the Mongolian was improved substantially for verb phrases and slightly for noun phrases by using POS information.

Test data	Khaltar and Fujii			Our method		
	Nouns	Verbs	Total	Nouns	Verbs	Total
News	85.5%	54.2%	70.0%	89.5%	84.4%	86.9%
Tech	84.8%	43.3%	75.2%	86.1%	88.0%	86.5%
Total	84.9%	48.9%	73.4%	86.9%	86.1%	86.6%

TABLE 2 – Accuracy of lemmatization by phrase types.

As shown in Table 2, the accuracy of the lemmatization on the noun and verb phrase types is improved for the both domain (News by 16.9% and Tech by 11.3%). In addition, we evaluated the performance of our method on the total tokens of the test data (Table 3). As a result, the total improvements are 9.2% on News and 10.6% on Tech.

Test data	Khaltar and Fujii			Our method		
	Nouns	Verbs	Total	Nouns	Verbs	Total
News	87.1%	75.1%	81.7%	91.0%	90.8%	90.9%
Tech	96.0%	60.1%	83.8%	96.9%	84.0%	92.5%
Total	94.5%	63.6%	82.9%	96.9%	85.6%	93.5%

TABLE 3 – Accuracy of lemmatization by phrase tokens.

As shown in Tables 2 and 3, the results of our method are higher than that of Khaltar and Fujii's method in the both of phrase types and phrase tokens.

We manually analyzed the errors in our method, and found seven types of errors in lemmatizing noun phrases (Table 4), and six types of errors in lemmatizing verb phrases (Table 5), respectively.

Error (# in News/Tech)	Examples	Correct
(a) Incorrect suffix removal (221/831)	дайнд → дай noun + dative in the war	дайн war
(b) Incorrect vowel insertion (139/719)	үнийг → үн noun + accusative price	үнэ price
(c) Soft sign insertion (9/198)	сургуулийн → сургуули noun + genitive of school	сургууль school
(d) Irregular plural suffix (108/116)	охид → охид noun + plural girls	охин girl
(e) Special possessive suffix (84/218)	ахынхаа → ахын noun + genitive + possessive my brother's	ах brother
(f) POS ambiguity (21/77)	орноос → ор noun + ablative from country	орон country
(h) Incorrect POS tagging (63/268)	угаар → уг noun smoke	угаар smoke

TABLE 4 – Errors of our method for noun phrases.

Error (# in News/Tech)	Example	Correct
(i) Incorrect suffix removal (302/236)	ярьжээ → ярьж verb + past told (to tell)	ярь to tell
(j) Incorrect vowel insertion (86/69)	идэвхжисэн → идэвхэж verb + past activated	идэвхж to active
(k) Soft sign insertion (9/7)	дэвшиж→дэвшь verb + serial verb suffix advanced	дэвш to advance
(l) Ignored by POS tagging (198/148)	авчихлаа → авчих verb + past perfect + past have just taken	ав to take
(m) POS ambiguity (11/13)	үрж → үр verb multiply	үрж multiply
(n) Incorrect POS tagging (100/83)	уудагийг → уудаг verb + present + accusative case that it drinks	уу to drink

TABLE 5 – Errors of our method for verb phrases.

As shown in Table 4, the most dominant errors in the noun phrase lemmatization are (a) and (b). Error (a) is a suffix homonym problem. In Mongolian, many suffixes are similar in their surface form, but different in their meaning or its opposite (similar in their meaning and different in their surface form). For resolving Error (a), only POS and syntactical function (such as cases, plural, etc) information is insufficient. It needs more detail lexical information to recognize the suffix boundaries. Error (b) is caused by the contradiction among the vowel insertion rules and the irregular concatenation form as well. In addition, Error (c) is similar to the Error (b). For correct vowel insertion needs more linguistic analysis for appropriate rule descriptions. Errors (d) and (e) can be resolved by simple heuristics. Error (d) needs a dictionary for irregular nouns while Error (e) can be solved by extending the segmentation rule. In the previous method, the segmentation rule did not consider the special possessive suffix.

Errors (f) and (h) are related to the POS tagging process. Although some cases of POS ambiguity (mentioned in the section 2) are solved in this work, there are other more ambiguous phrases, which the POS tagging in this work is not enough to resolve. Furthermore, the incorrect POS tagged phrases lead to the inappropriate lemmatization process as causing the error (h).

As shown in Table 5, errors from (i) to (k) are the same problems as in the noun errors. The errors from (l) to (n) are related to the POS tagging. Errors (m) and (n) are also the same errors in the noun lemmatization while Error (l) is caused by that the POS tagging used in this work ignores some inflectional functions of verbs. As a result, such verb suffixes are not removed.

4.3 Evaluating the contribution of lemmatization to SMT

In this experiment, we evaluated the effectiveness of our lemmatization method for English-Mongolian (En-Mn) phrase-based SMT. Khaltar and Fujii's method was also evaluated for comparison. We used Moses (Koehn et al., 2007) with the standard configuration and GIZA++ (Och et al., 2003) with the grow-diag-final-and heuristic for word-alignment. Our parallel data set was collected from web sites (http://www.legalinfo.mn/ and http://mongolia.usembassy.gov/), and consists of law and news domains. Example En-Mn sentence pairs in our data are shown below.

En1: Occupational safety and health measures shall not involve any expenditure for the workers .
Mn1: Хөдөлмөрийн аюулгүй байдал , эрүүл ахуйн арга хэмжээтэй холбогдох аливаа зардлыг ажилчид хариуцахгүй .

En2: Agriculture even holds a key to delivering new forms of clean energy .
Mn2: Үүнтэй зэрэгцээд хөдөө аж ахуй нь цэвэр эрчим хүчний шинэ төрлийг бий болгоход ч голлох үүрэг гүйцэтгэж байна .

The numbers of sentence pairs for training a translation model, tuning parameters, and testing were 24 K, 2 K, and 500, respectively. We used SRILM (Stolcke et al., 2011) and a 5-gram word language model in Mongolian was produced from 106 K sentences in Mongolian.

We compared two types of SMT methods for English-Mongolian: an SMT with lemmatization for noun and verb phrases in Mongolian (WL) and an SMT without lemmatization (WOL). We used BLEU (Papineniet al., 2002) for evaluation purposes. While translations in Mongolian produced by WL were lemmatized inherently, translations by WOL and reference translations were not lemmatized. To compare BLEU values for WOL and WL strictly, we segmented the translations by WOL and the reference translations using the same lemmatization method as WL. Table 6 shows BLEU values for different SMT methods.

WOL1	38.74
Khaltar and Fujii	38.43
WOL2	39.11
Our method	40.48

TABLE 6 – BLEU values for different SMT methods.

In Table 6, there are four SMT methods. Two of them are WLs ("Khaltar and Fujii" and "Our method") and the remaining methods are WOL1 and WOL2. While our lemmatization method was used in "Our method" and the output of WOL2, Khaltar and Fujii's method was used in "Khaltar and Fujii" and the output of WOL1. Looking at Table 6, the BLEU value for Khaltar and Fujii's method was smaller than that for WOL1. In other words, Khaltar and Fujii's method was not effective in terms of SMT. However, the BLEU value for our method was greater than that for WOL2. In addition, we performed a statistical testing (Koehn, 2004) and found that the difference between our method and WOL2 in BLEU was statistically significant with the 95% confidence level. We can conclude that our lemmatization for Mongolian was effective for English-Mongolian SMT.

Conclusion

In this paper, we proposed a lemmatization method, which identifies the original form of the content word in a Cyrillic Mongolian phrase. Although the state-of-the-art method does not need a noun dictionary and is therefore scalable, this method incorrectly lemmatizes out-of-dictionary verbs and words associated with more than one part of speech (POS). To resolve this problem, our method first performs statistical POS tagging for an input phrase and then performs the lemmatization. To evaluate the effectiveness of our method, we targeted noun and verb phrases in newspaper articles and technical abstracts. Experimental results showed that our method substantially improved the accuracy of the state-of-the-art lemmatization method. We also applied our lemmatization method to English-Mongolian SMT and showed that our lemmatization method improved BLEU values for SMT experimentally.

Future work includes improving lemmatization rules for special noun possessive suffixes and a dictionary for irregular plural nouns. In addition, more linguistic analysis is necessary for statistically resolving the vowel insertion and the suffix homonym problems. Further research is necessary to obtain more improvement over English-Mongolian SMT. It needs to determine the effective phrases for the segmentation of Mongolian.

References

Thorsten Brants (2000). *TnT – A Statistical Part-of-Speech Tagger*, In Proceedings of the Sixth Applied Natural Language Processing Conference.

Terumasa Ehara, Suzushi Hayata, and Nobuyuki Kimura (2007). *Mongolian to Japanese Machine Translation System – Focused on Translation Selection*, In Proceedings of the 2nd International Symposium on Information and Language Processing.

Antworth Evan (1990). *PC-KIMMO: A Two-level Processor for Morphological Analysis*, Summer Institute of Linguistics, Inc.

Purev Jaimai and Odbayar Chimeddorj (2008). *POS Tagging for Mongolian, In Proceedings of Sixth Workshop on Asian Language Processing*, IJCNLP2008.

Purev Jaimai, Tsolmon Zundui, Altangerel Chagnaa, and Cheol-Young Ock (2005). *PC-KIMMO-based Description of Mongolian Morphology*, In Proceeding of International Journal of Information Processing Systems, Vol. 1, No.1.

Badam-Osor Khaltar and Atsushi Fujii (2009). *A Lemmatization method for Mongolian and its application to indexing for information retrieval*, Information Processing & Management, Vol. 45, No.4, pp.438-451.

Philipp Koehn (2007). *Statistical Significance Tests for Machine Translation Evaluation*. In the Proceedings of the 2004 Conference on Empirical Methods in Natural Language Processing, Barcelona, Spain.

Philipp Koehn, Hieu Hoang, Alexandra Birch, Chris Callison-Burch, Marcello Federico, Nicola Bertoldi, Brooke Cowan, Wade Shen, Christine Moran, Richard Zens, Chris Dyer, Ondrej Bojar, Alexandra Constantin, and Evan Herbst (2007). *Moses: Open source toolkit for statistical machine translation*. In Proceedings of the 45th Annual Meeting of the ACL, Demonstration session, Prague, Czech Republic.

Koskenniemi Kimmo (1983). *Two-level morphology: a general computational model for word-form recognition and production*, Publication No. 11. Helsinki: University of Helsinki Department of General Linguistics.

Franz Josef Och, Hermann Ney (2003). *A Systematic Comparison of Various Statistical Alignment Models*, Computational Linguistics, volume 29, number 1, pp. 19-51.

Kishore Papineni, Salim Roukos, Todd Ward, and Wei-Jing Zhu. (2002). *Bleu: a method for automatic evaluation of machine translation*. In Proceedings of ACL2002, pages 311–318, Philadelphia, Pennsylvania.

Enkhbayar Sanduijav, Takehito Utsuro, and Satoshi Sato (2005). *Mongolian phrase generation and morphological analysis based on phonological and morphological constraints*, Journal of Natural Language Processing, Vol. 12, No. 5, pp.185-205. (In Japanese).

Andreas Stolcke, Jing Zheng, Wen Wang and Victor Abrash (2011). *SRILM at Sixteen: Update and Outlook*. In Proceedings of IEEE Automatic Speech Recognition and Understanding Workshop, Waikoloa, Hawaii.

Translations of Ambiguous Hindi Pronouns to Possible Bengali Pronouns

Sanjay Chatterji, Arnab Dhar, Sudeshna Sarkar, Anupam Basu
Department of Computer Sc. & Engineering, Indian Institute of Technology, Kharagpur, India
Email: {schatt,arnabdhar,sudeshna,anupam}@cse.iitkgp.ernet.in

ABSTRACT

In a Hindi to Bengali transfer based machine translation system the baseline lexical transfer module replaces a Hindi word by its most frequent Bengali translation. Some pronouns in Hindi can have multiple translations in Bengali. The choices of actual translations have big impact on the accessibility of the translated sentence. The list of Hindi pronouns is small and their corresponding Bengali translations may be judged using a set of rules. In this paper, we are working on the translations of ambiguous Hindi pronouns to possible Bengali pronouns. We observed the uses of Hindi pronouns in a Hindi corpus and formulated the translation rules based on their translations in parallel Bengali corpus.

1 Introduction

Hindi and Bengali both originated from Old Indo-Aryan family of languages and are similar in structure. They have lot of similarities even though there are differences in the form of uses and positions of the words in corresponding sentences. According to Koul (2008), Hindi pronouns can be broadly categorized into seven types namely, Personal, Demonstrative, Indefinite, Relative-Correlative, Possessive, Interrogative and Reflexive. Among these Hindi pronouns some are used both as Personal, Demonstrative, and Relative-Correlative pronouns. In Bengali, there are different pronouns for each of these uses. As the list of Hindi such pronouns is small and their uses are limited, it is possible to differentiate each use and find their Bengali translations using a set of linguistic rules.

In a transfer based machine translation system source language words and phrases are transferred to suitable target language words and phrases. A baseline lexical transfer module transfers words and phrases to their most frequent translations. If a word is ambiguous then the module which finds its sense in the current context is referred to as Word Sense Disambiguator (WSD). Word sense disambiguation can be done using statistical and rule based approaches. Identifying uses of pronouns is one of the WSD tasks.

In this paper, we propose rules for disambiguating ambiguous Hindi pronouns which will be translated to different Bengali pronouns in different constructs. We have developed these rules by analysing the sentences in a large Hindi corpus taken from Hindi story books, newspapers, web etc. and their translations in the parallel Bengali corpus. The rules are discussed with example Hindi sentences and their corresponding Bengali translations. The effects of the rules applied in the Hindi to Bengali transfer based Machine Translation (MT) system are evaluated and analysed.

2 Related Work

The correlative clauses in Hindi correlative constructions are discussed and analysed by Bhatt (2003), Kachru (1973), Srivastav (1991), Dayal (1996), etc. They have given extensive study on the use of Dem-XP adjunction structures (a noun phrase headed by a demonstrative pronoun) in the correlative constructions. Similar correlative clauses are also available in Bengali as discussed by Dasgupta (1980), Bagchi (1994), etc.

Dash (2000) has developed a system to identify and analyse Bengali pronouns in corpus data. They have explored the morphological structure of Bengali pronouns in the corpus. The morphological structures of Bengali words (including pronouns) are also analysed by Bhattacharya et al. (2005). Prasad (2000) have investigated the uses of Hindi pronouns in corpus data.

A few attempts have been made in formatting rules for translating pronouns for some language pairs. For example, Patel and Pareek (2010) have analysed the influence of grammatical properties in the translation of Hindi words (including pronouns) to Gujarati.

Some work has been done on the analysis of the pronouns which are used as anaphora in Hindi and Bengali languages. A shared task has been carried out on anaphora resolution on these languages in ICON 2011 and the results of the participants are discussed in Sobha et al. (2011).

3 Translation Rules for Ambiguous Hindi Pronouns

Most of the Hindi pronouns have single translation in Bengali. Some of such pronouns which occur frequently in the corpus are listed in Table 1 with the corresponding Bengali translations. The transliteration into Roman using Itrans and English translations of these examples are also included.

Hindi Pronoun	**Bengali Translation**	**English Translation**	**Hindi Pronoun**	**Bengali Translation**	**English Translation**
मैं (mai.N)	আমি (Ami)	I	कौन(kauna)	কে (ke)	who
तू (tu)	তুই (tui)	you-familiar	क्या (kyA)	কি (ki)	what
तुम(tuma)	তুমি (tumi)	you-normal	कब (kaba)	কখন(kakhana)	when
आप (Apa)	আপনি(Apani)	you-formal	तब (taba)	তখন(takhana)	then

TABLE 1 – List of some Hindi pronouns that have single translations in Bengali.

Some Hindi pronouns are used to demonstrate both animate and inanimate nouns and as third person personal pronouns. For these three uses a single Hindi pronoun is used where in Bengali there are dedicated pronouns for each use. Given such a Hindi pronoun, we have to find its use in the corresponding sentence and translate it to corresponding Bengali pronoun. In this paper, we consider three such pronouns namely यह (yaha), बह (baha), and जो (jo) and identify their translation rules.

Unlike Hindi, in certain cases classifiers are added to Bengali nouns and pronouns. We discuss the rules of adding the classifiers and case markers (suffixes) with the Bengali translations of the Hindi pronouns.

3.1 Handling यह (yaha)

Three different constructions of the Hindi pronoun यह (yaha) are shown below.

1. The noun being demonstrated is present in the surface.
2. The noun being demonstrated is absent and the absent noun is inanimate.
3. The noun being demonstrated is absent and the absent noun is animate. In this case, the pronoun is usually a third person personal pronoun.

In the first two cases the corresponding Bengali pronoun is এই (ei). The singular classifiers টা (TA) or টি (Ti), the plural classifiers গুলো (gulo) or গুলি (guli), and the case markers (র (ra), কে (ke), তে (te), etc) are added with the Bengali nouns being demonstrated in the first case and with the Bengali pronouns in the second case where the noun is not present in the surface.

In the third case the corresponding Bengali pronoun is এ (e). In this case, as the noun indicated by the pronoun does not follow it in the surface, the pronoun can be considered as personal pronoun. However, the features of the noun to which the pronoun is indicating is used when translated in Bengali. The singular classifier 0 (Zero) and the plural classifier রা (rA) is added with this pronoun when the indicated noun is animate. The Bengali pronoun এই (ei) is used when the indicated noun is inanimate and the singular classifiers টা (TA) or টি (Ti) and the plural classifiers গুলো (gulo) or গুলি (guli) are added with it.

Example sentences for each construction of this Hindi pronoun and their translations in Bengali and English are shown in Table 2.

Hindi Pronoun	Us-es	Hindi Example	Bengali Translation	English Translation
यह (yaha)	1	यह लड़का मेरा भाइ है। (yaha la.DakA merA bhAi hai.)	এই ছেলেটা আমার ভাই। (ei chheleTA AmAra bhAi.)	This boy is my brother.
	2	यह मेरा है। (yaha merA hai.)	এইটা আমার। (eiTA AmAra.)	This is mine.
	3	यह कौन है? (yaha kauna hai.)	এ কে? (e ke?)	Who is he?

TABLE 2 – Examples of different constructions of Hindi pronoun यह (yaha).

3.2 Handling बह (baha) in simple construction

The Hindi pronoun बह (baha) has the similar constructions as mentioned in Section 3.1. The rules of adding the classifiers and case markers are also similar. In the first two cases the corresponding Bengali pronoun is ওই (oi) and in the third case the corresponding Bengali pronoun is ও (o). Example sentences for each construction of this Hindi pronoun and their translations in Bengali and English are shown in Table 3.

Hindi Pronoun	Us-es	Hindi Example	Bengali Translation	English Translation
बह (baha)	1	बह घर मेरा है। (baha ghara merA hai.)	ওই বাড়িটা আমার। (oi bA.DiTA AmAra.)	That home is mine.
	2	बह मेरा है। (baha merA hai.)	ওইটা আমার। (oiTA AmAra.)	That is mine.
	3	बह या रहा है। (baha yA rahA hai.)	ও যাচ্ছে। (o yAchchhe.)	He is going.

TABLE 3 – Examples of different constructions of Hindi pronoun बह (baha).

3.3 Handling जो (jo) - बह (baha) in relative-correlative construction

The Hindi relative pronoun जो (jo) and the Hindi correlative pronoun बह (baha) have the similar constructions as mentioned in Section 3.1. The rules of adding the classifiers and case markers are also similar. In the first two cases the Bengali translations of these pronouns are যেই (yei) and সেই (sei) and in the third case these are যে (ye) and সে (se), respectively. In the third case when the Bengali plural classifier রা (rA) is added with the pronouns then the orthographic changes are যে+রা = যারা (ye+rA=yArA) and সে+রা = তারা (se+rA=tArA). Example sentences for each of these constructions for Hindi pronouns जो (jo) and बह (baha) and their translations in Bengali and English are shown in Table 4.

Hindi Pronoun	Us-es	Hindi Example	Bengali Translation	English Translation
जो (jo) and बह (baha)	1	जो घर मेरा है बह घर तेरा भी है। (jo ghara merA hai baha ghara terA bhI hai.)	যেই বাড়িটা আমার সেই বাড়িটা তোরও। (yei bA.DiTA AmAra sei bA.DiTA torao.)	My home is your home too.
	2	जो बोल रहा हुं बह करो। (jo bola rahA hu.N baha karo.)	যেইটা বলছি সেইটা করো। (yeiTA balachhi seiTA karo.)	Do what I am telling.
	3	जो खड़ा है बह मेरा भाई है। (jo kha.DA hai baha merA bhAi hai.)	যে দাঁড়িয়ে আছে সে আমার ভাই। (ye d.NA.DiYe Achhe se AmAra bhAi.)	Who is standing is my brother.

TABLE 4 – Examples of different constructions of Hindi pronouns जो (jo) and बह (baha)

The Hindi relative pronoun जो (jo) is sometimes followed by कुछ (kUchha), सब (saba), etc. to indicate an abstract amount of things. In these cases the pronoun is translated to Bengali pronoun যা (yA). An example of such construction is given below.

जो कुछ मैंने माँगा है बह सब मिला है। (jo kUchha mai.Nne mA.ngA hai baha saba milA hai.)
যা কিছু আমি চেয়েছি সেই সব পেয়েছি। (yA kichhu Ami cheYechhi sei saba peYechhi.)

Those which I wanted I got.

According to Section 3.2 and the current section, different translations of Hindi pronoun बह (baha) and its inflected forms are shown in Table 5. Each empty cell indicates that the corresponding inflected form does not have the corresponding construction.

	बह (baha)	उस (usa)	उसका (usakA)	बो (bo)
Simple 1	ওই (oi)	ওই (oi)		ওই (oi)
Simple 2	ওইটা (oiTA)		ওইটার(oiTAra)	
Simple 3	ও (o)		ওর (ora)	উনি (uni)
Correlative 1	সেই (sei)	সেই (sei)		সেই (sei)
Correlative 2	সেইটা(seiTA)		সেইটার(seiTAra)	
Correlative 3	সে (se)		তার (tAra)	তিনি (tini)

TABLE 5 – Translations of different forms of बह (baha)

3.4 Handling Hindi pronominal suffixes

Hindi nominal suffixes को (ko), का (kA), से (se), पे (pe), etc. are also used with Hindi pronouns. Different uses of these Hindi pronominal suffixes have different Bengali translations. The most frequent corresponding Bengali pronominal suffixes are কে (ke), র (ra), থেকে (theke), এ (e), etc. The suffixes which have different translations can be disambiguated with the help of rules.

We have identified the rules of translating the pronominal Hindi suffix को (ko) as discussed below. Then, the rules for translating the Hindi suffix से (se) are discussed.

The Hindi pronouns इसे (ise) and इसको (isako) as well as the Hindi pronouns उसे (use) and उसको (usako) are used interchangeably. Now, इसे (ise) and उसे (use) Hindi pronouns have different Bengali translations for the following two different cases.

1. If these pronouns indicate the things or persons to whom something is told, given, etc. then their corresponding translations are একে (eke) and ওকে (oke). In this case the Hindi word इसे (ise) is यह्+को (yaha+ko) and उसे (use) is बह्+को (baha+ko). The corresponding Bengali translations are এ+কে (e+ke) and ও+কে (o+ke), respectively.
2. If these pronouns indicate the things (inanimate) which are being kept, given, etc. then their corresponding translations are এইটা (eiTA) (alternatively এইটাকে (eiTAke)) and ওইটা (oiTA) (alternatively ওইটাকে (oiTAke)). In this case the Hindi word इसे (ise) is यह्+0 (yaha+0) and उसे (use) is बह्+0 (baha+0). The corresponding Bengali translations are এই+টা (ei+TA) and ওই+টা (oi+TA).

The noun being indicated by these two pronouns can be animate or inanimate in the first case and are inanimate in the second case. Examples for each of these two uses of

Hindi pronouns and their translations in Bengali and English are shown in Table 6.

Case	Hindi Example	Bengali Translation	English Translation
1	इसलिए इसे ब्रह्मकुंड कहा याता है। (isalie ise brahmaku.nDa kahA yAtA hai.) इसलिए उसे डांटता हूँ। (isalie use DA.nTatA hu.N.)	এইজন্য একে ব্রহ্মকুন্ড বলা হয় । (eijanya eke brahmakuNDa balA haYa.) এইজন্য ওকে বকি । (eijanya oke baki.)	That's why it is called Brahmakund. That's why I scold him.
2	इसे तुम रख लो। (ise tuma rakha lo.) उसे ठीक से रखो। (use Thika se rakho.)	এইটা তুমি রেখে দাও । (eiTA tumi rekhe dAo.) ওইটা ঠিক করে রাখো । (oiTA Thika kare rAkho.)	Keep it with you. Keep that carefully.

TABLE 6 – Examples of different uses of Hindi pronouns इसे (ise) and उसे (use).

The Hindi pronoun उसे (use) is also used as correlative pronoun and then its Bengali translations are তাকে (tAke) and সেইটা (seiTA) (alternatively সেইটাকে (seiTAke)) for these two cases, respectively.

The Hindi pronominal suffix or postposition से (se) can be translated to different Bengali suffixes and postpositions similar to the case on noun as discussed in Mukhopadhyay et al. (2008). Following are some examples of Hindi pronoun उससे (usase) (बह+से (baha+se)) and its translations in Bengali and English, respectively.

उससे कुछ्र मत कहो। (usase kuchha mata kaho.)
ওকে কিছু বোলো না । (oke kichhu bolo nA.)
Don't tell him anything.

उससे कुछ्र ही दुरी पर मेरा घर है। (usase kuchha hI durI para merA ghara hai.)
ওখান থেকে কিছু দূরেই আমার ঘর । (okhAna theke kichhu durei AmAra ghara.)
My home is near to that place.

यह घर उससे बना हुआ है। (yaha ghara usase banA huA hai.)
এই ঘরটা ওইটা দিয়ে বানানো । (ei gharaTA oiTA diYe bAnAno.)
This home is made of that.

3.5 Handling इस (isa), उस (usa), यहाँ (yahA.N) and उहाँ (uhA.N)

There are some pronouns which are translated differently when they occur as inflected form in the surface. The Hindi pronouns इस (isa) and उस (usa) are used as demonstrative pronouns when they are not inflected and then their Bengali translations are এই (ei) and ওই (oi), respectively. When they are inflected, then the roots are translated as এ (e) and ও (o), respectively.

Similarly, the Hindi pronouns यहाँ (yahA.N) and उहाँ (uhA.N) are translated to Bengali pronouns এখানে (ekhAne) and ওখানে (okhAne) when they are not inflected and to Bengali pronouns এখান (ekhAna) and ওখান (okhAna) when they are inflected.

The examples of uses of such pronouns are shown below with Bengali and English translations. In the first example, first उस (usa) is not inflected and second उस (usa) is inflected and the corresponding translations are ওই (oi) and ও (o), respectively. In the second example, first उहाँ (uhA.N) is inflected and second उहाँ (uhA.N) is not inflected and the corresponding translations are ওখান (okhAna) and ওখানে (okhAne), respectively.

> उस लड़के को **उसके** बारे में मत बोलो | (usa la.Dake ko usake bAre me.n mata bolo.)
> ওই ছেলেটাকে ওর সম্বন্ধে বোলো না । (oi chheleTAke ora sambandhe bolo nA.)
> Don't tell that boy about him.
>
> (**उहाँ से**) उहाँ याओ | (uhA.N se uhA.N yAo.)
> **ওখান** থেকে **ওখানে** যাও । (okhAna theke okhAne yAo.)
> Go from there to there.

4 Implementation

To apply the rules for translating Hindi pronouns to Bengali it is important to decide whether the noun being demonstrated is present in the surface and to identify the animacy (whether animate or inanimate) of the demonstrated nouns. Based on these observations and the suffix value given by the Hindi morphological analyzer we translate them using the proposed rules.

4.1 Identifying Animacy

If the demonstrated noun is absent, then the animacy is not implicit. In this case, generally, the verb and the dependency relations provide the clue. The subjects (karta) of some activities like खाना (khAnA), खेलना (khelanA), etc. are animate and their objects (karma) are inanimate. The indirect objects (gauna karma) of some activities like बोलना (bolanA), देना (denA), etc. are animate and their direct objects (mukhya karma) are inanimate. We have listed 2 such types of verbs to identify the animacy.

Sometimes we get the animacy information from other nouns or pronouns. The animacy of the noun of proposition (samanadhikaran) is same as the animacy of the corresponding subject (karta). Hindi question words also contain the animacy information which is same as the animacy of the corresponding subjects (karta). For example, कौन (kauna) is animate and क्या (kyA) is inanimate Hindi question words. We have copied the animacy features based on these agreements.

4.2 Deciding whether the demonstrated noun is present in the surface

Generally, if the demonstrated noun is present then it will immediately follow the pronoun. Sometimes, the demonstrative pronoun and the demonstrated noun are intervened by some adjectives. However, the nouns followed by these pronouns are not always the ones being demonstrated. In the following examples, the noun घर(ghara) is not being demonstrated. We hypothesize that if the immediately followed noun is not inflected (except pluralized) and no verb or conjunct immediately follow that noun then that noun is being demonstrated. We have implemented the decision module based on this hypothesis.

यह घर नहीं है| (yaha ghara nahI.N hai.)	यह घर का दरबाजा है| (yaha ghara kA darabAjA hai.)
এইটা বাড়ি নয়। (eiTA bA.Di naYa.)	এইটা বাড়ির দরজা। (eiTA bA.Dira darajA.)
This is not a home.	This is the door of the home.

5 Evaluation

We have used 100 Hindi sentences for testing the proposed rules. We are considering personal and demonstrative pronouns. There are 129 such pronouns in these test sentences. Out of them 19 are unique roots and remaining are the inflections of these 19 roots. The detailed analyses of translations of pronouns are discussed below.

5.1 Analysis

The baseline transfer based MT system replaces these pronouns by their most frequent translations. Among 129 pronouns 103 pronouns are translated correctly by this baseline system. Then, the rules proposed in this paper are used as the transfer grammar rules in this baseline system. The 103 correct translations of the baseline system are also translated correctly by the modified system. Among other 26 other translations 21 are modified correctly (total 124 correct translations) using the rules and 5 are either not modified or the modification is also incorrect.

Examples of input Hindi sentences from the 100 test sentences and their Bengali translations using the baseline and modified systems are shown and discussed below. Correct modifications are made boldface and others are underlined.

1. **Hindi Input:** जो पुण्य ब्रह्मकुंड में स्नान से मिलता है, वह कहीं नहीं मिलता है। (jo puNya brahmaku.nDa me.n snAna se milatA hai, baha kahI.n nahI.n milatA hai.)
   English Translation: The favour you will get by bathing in Brahmakunda, that is not available anywhere.
   Baseline Output: **যা** পুণ্য ব্রহ্মকুণ্ডে স্নান থেকে মেলে, **সে** কোথাও মেলে না। (yA puNya brahmakunDe snAna theke mele, se kothAo mele nA.)
   Modified Output: **যেই** পুণ্য ব্রহ্মকুণ্ডে স্নান থেকে মেলে, **সেইটা** কোথাও মেলে না। (yei puNya brahmakunDe snAna theke mele, seiTA kothAo mele nA.)

2. **Hindi Input:** जो भी भक्त इन मंदिरों में दर्शन हेतु आते हैं, वे **इनसे** पूजा जरूर करवाते हैं। (jo bhI bhakta ina ma.ndiro.n me.n darshana hetu Ate hai.n, be inase pUjA jarUra karabAte hai.n.)
   English Translation: Whoever followers come in this temple for holy witness, those definitely worship by him.
   Baseline Output: যাও ভক্ত এ মন্দিরে দর্শনের জন্য আসে, তারা এর_**থেকে** পূজা নিঃসন্দেহে করায়। (yAo bhakta e mandire darshanera janya Ase, tArA era_theke pUjA niHsandehe karAYa.)
   Modified Output: যেইও ভক্ত এই মন্দিরে দর্শনের জন্য আসে, তারা **একে_দিয়ে** পূজা নিঃসন্দেহে করায়। (yeio bhakta ei mandire darshanera janya Ase, tArA eke_diYe pUjA niHsandehe karAYa.)

5.2 Evaluation of Effect of Rules in Machine Translation

The translations of the 100 sentences by the baseline and the modified MT systems are used for automatic evaluation. Three reference translations are used to calculate the BLEU and NIST scores. The averages of three scores with respect to three different reference translations are shown in Table 7.

	BLEU	NIST
Baseline MT system	0.1660	4.2142
Modified MT system	0.1669	4.2514

TABLE 7 – BLEU and NIST scores of the Baseline and Modified MT systems.

6 Conclusion

The problems in machine translation can be handled by capturing comprehensive and unified rules for different categories of words. This process is lengthy for some class of words like noun, verb, etc. where there are a large number of ambiguities. But the class of words in which the number of ambiguity is limited, there the rules may be helpful. For example, the proposed rules for translating ambiguous Hindi pronouns to Bengali may be implemented easily to solve the pronominal ambiguities.

The statistical way of learning the rules for each category is a quick solution for the overall translation problems. The automatically learned rules for translation of Hindi pronouns to Bengali can be compared with these manually created rules in future. The effect of these rules in other applications like, anaphora resolution, question answering, etc. should also be tested in future.

Acknowledgement

This work is partially supported by the ILMT project sponsored by TDIL program of MCIT, Govt. of India. We would like to thank all the members in Communication Empowerment Lab, IIT Kharagpur.

References

Bagchi, T. (1994). *Bangla Correlative Pronouns, Relative Clause Order and D-Linking*, in M. Butt, T. H. King, and G. Ramchand (eds.), Theoretical Perspectives on Word Order in South Asian Languages, CSLI Lecture Notes, No. 50, CSLI, Stanford, California, pp. 13–30.

Bhatt, R. (2003). *Locality in Correlatives.* In Natural Language & Linguistic Theory, Vol. 21, No. 3, pp. 485–541.

Bhattacharya, S., Choudhury, M., Sarkar, S., and Basu, A. (2005). *Inflectional morphology synthesis for Bengali noun, pronoun and verb systems*, in Proceedings of the national conference on computer processing of Bangla (NCCPB), pp. 34–43.

Dash, N. S. (2000). *Bangla Pronouns - a Corpus Based Study.* In Literary and Linguistic Computing, Vol. 15, No. 4, pp. 433-443.

Dasgupta, P. (1980). *Questions and Relative and Complement Clauses in a Bangla Grammar.* unpublished Ph.D. dissertation, New York University.

Dayal, V. (1996). *Locality in Wh-Quantification: Questions and Relative Clauses in Hindi.* Studies in Linguistics and Philosophy, No. 62, Kluwer, Dordrecht.

Kachru, Y. (1973). *Some Aspects of Pronominalization and Relative Clause Construction in Hindi-Urdu,* in B. B. Kachru (ed.), Papers on South Asian Linguistics, Vol. 3.2, Studies in the Linguistic Sciences, Department of Linguistics, University of Illinois, Urbana, pp. 87–103.

Koul, O. N. (2008). *Book Title: Modern Hindi Grammar.* Dunwoody Press, Springfield, VA 22150, USA.

Mukhopadhyay, S., Barik, B., and Sarkar, S. (2008). *Problems of Transfer Grammar: The Hindi Postpositional Correlatives in Bangla.* In Proceedings of 6th International Conference on Natural Language Processing (ICON 2008), Pune, India.

Patel, K. A., and Pareek, J. S. (2010). *Rule base to resolve translation problems due to differences in gender properties in sibling language pair Gujarati-Hindi.* In Proceedings of Computer and Communication Technology (ICCCT), pp.776-781.

Prasad, R. (2000). *A Corpus Study of Zero Pronouns in Hindi: An Account Based on Centering Transition Preferences.* In Proceedings of DAARC 2000, Discourse Anaphora and Reference Resolution Conference. Lancaster University, 66-71.

Sobha, L., Bandyopadhyay, S., Ram, V. S., and A., Akiladeswari. (2011). *NLP Tool Contest @ICON2011 on Anaphora Resolution in Indian Languages.* In Proceedings of ICON2011 NLP Tools Contest: Anaphora Resolution in Indian Languages, Chennai, India.

Srivastav, V. (1991). *The Syntax and Semantics of Correlatives.* Natural Language and Linguistic Theory 9, pp. 637–686.

Author Index

Alok, Deepak, 105
Analoui, Morteza, 45
Anwar, Waqas, 95

Bajwa, Usama Ijaz, 95
Barik, Biswanath, 65
Barman, Anup Kr, 21
Barman, Anup Kr., 29
Basu, Anupam, 55, 65, 125
Bharali, Himadri, 21
Bhatt, Brijesh, 75
Bhattacharyya, Pushpak, 75
Boro, Bhatima, 29
Brahma, Biswajit, 29

Cahyadi, Denny, 85
Chatterji, Sanjay, 55, 65, 125
Choi, Key-Sun, 1
Cromieres, Fabien, 85

Datta, Nabanita, 65
Deka, Ratul, 21
Dhar, Arnab, 55, 65

Fujii, Atsushi, 115

Gogoi, Ambeswar, 21

Hahm, YoungGyun, 1
He, Yeping, 11

Jahangir, Faryal, 95

Kumar, Ritesh, 105
Kurohashi, Sadao, 85

Lahiri, Bornini, 105
Lim, KyungTae, 1
Liu, Huidan, 11

Megyesi, Beáta, 35

Nivre, Joakim, 35
Nuo, Minghua, 11

Odbayar, Chimeddorj, 115

Park, Jungyeul, 1

Sarabi, Zahra, 45
Sarkar, Sudeshna, 55, 65, 125
Sarma, Prof. Shikhar Kr., 21, 29
Seraji, Mojgan, 35

Wang, Xuan, 95
Wu, Jian, 11

Yoon, Yongun, 1

Association for Computational Linguistics
209 N. Eighth Street
Stroudsburg, Pennsylvania 18360

CURRAN ASSOCIATES INC
proceedings.com

Student Research Workshop

(RANLPStud 2013)

Associated with the 9th International Conference on Recent Advances in Natural Language Processing (RANLP 2013)

Hissar, Bulgaria
9 – 11 September 2013

ISBN: 978-1-62993-556-0